# Fast Boats and Fast Times
Memories of a PT Boat Skipper in the South Pacific

by

David M. Levy and Gerald A. Meehl

authorHOUSE®

*AuthorHouse*™
*1663 Liberty Drive, Suite 200*
*Bloomington, IN 47403*
*www.authorhouse.com*
*Phone: 1-800-839-8640*

*This book is a work of non-fiction. Unless otherwise noted, the authors and the publisher make no explicit guarantees as to the accuracy of the information contained in this book and in some cases, names of people and places have been altered to protect their privacy.*

*First published by AuthorHouse 7/28/2008*

*ISBN: 978-1-4389-0017-9 (sc)*
*ISBN: 978-1-4389-0018-6 (hc)*

*Library of Congress Control Number: 2008906041*

*Printed in the United States of America*
*Bloomington, Indiana*

*This book is printed on acid-free paper.*

# CONTENTS

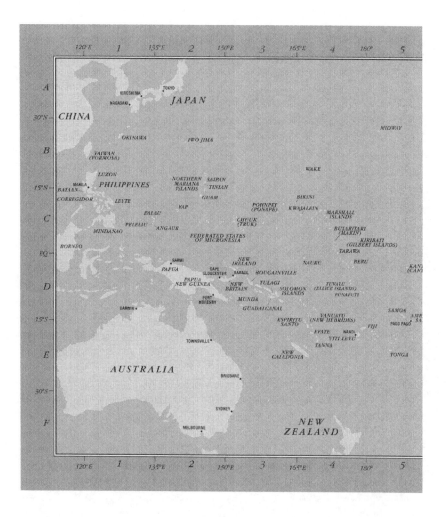

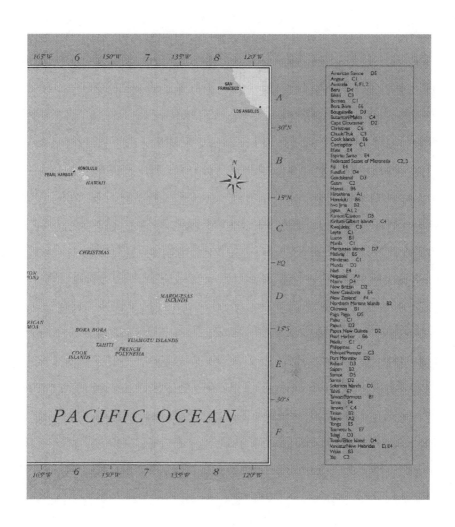

# FOREWORD

*February 8, 1943*

Two powerful American patrol-torpedo boats were moving slowly along the tropical west coast of Guadalcanal, a large island of the Solomons chain in the southwest Pacific. It was about 2 a.m., and very dark. The boats were going single file, with Hugh "Big Robbie" Robinson at the wheel of the boat in front, and Dave "Hogan" Levy, skipper of PT 59, following close behind. Both men were wearing headphones connected to their boat's radio, and each was holding a microphone to his mouth. The other hand grasped the small steering wheel in the open cockpit of each 77-foot-long wooden boat. Robinson and Levy talked by radio back and forth, staying in constant contact, to make sure their boats stuck close together. They were feeling their way cautiously along the black shoreline of the island and could barely make out against the sky the imposing jungle trees that pressed down to a narrow beach. The muffled exhaust from three big Packard V-12 engines in each boat bubbled up from under the stern, the engines idling in a constrained rumble. The boats continued to proceed slowly, not only because it was dark but also to minimize the glow of phosphorescence churned up by their wakes. Slow-flying Japanese floatplanes, launched from enemy cruisers, also patrolled the Guadalcanal coast at night. They were looking for American boats to attack, and the telltale signs of a glowing wake would point like an arrow to a torpedo boat. The sailors in the PT boat crews were all at battle stations, tensely hunched over machine guns or torpedo tubes, straining to hear any sound or see any indication of enemy troops on shore.

Levy and Robinson had been assigned patrol duty that night, to be on the lookout for any attempts by Japanese ships to evacuate their imperiled forces from their original positions on the far side of Guadalcanal. The American PT boats had been going out on nerve-wracking night patrols for almost three months. They repeatedly engaged and harassed the "Tokyo Express," their name for the convoys of Japanese warships sent to shell Henderson Field, the American-held airstrip on Guadalcanal, and the Marine units defending it, as well as to re-supply their own troops on the island. Some nights the PT boats patrolled in pitch darkness and didn't see a thing. Other nights Japanese destroyers or cruisers would suddenly materialize out of the blackness. The small boats would move in close to launch their torpedoes and then leave in a big hurry, weaving violently side to side to dodge the rain of large-caliber gunfire from the Japanese warships. There were explosions heard, but it was always difficult to determine what the torpedoes might have hit, with muzzle flashes from enemy ships mixing in with shells exploding all around the speeding PT boats. The Japanese tried to keep their searchlights trained on the small, fleeing crafts, but if the boats sped away too fast, Japanese gunners could still spot their phosphorescent wakes and zero in on their targets. Robinson had had the bow of his original boat, PT 61, blown away as he tried to outrun a Japanese destroyer in hot pursuit. The shell that hit the boat had zoomed over his shoulder from behind and exploded on the uplifted bow, as the boat's powerful Packard engines dug the stern into the water at speeds approaching 45 miles per hour. Other

PT boats had been blown completely out of the water in trying to evade the deadly firepower of larger Japanese ships, their crews killed or wounded.

Levy had launched his torpedoes during such confused engagements in previous months, but never knew if he had hit anything in the subsequent chaos of explosions and muzzle flashes that seared the night sky like strobe lights in a darkened room.

The U.S. Marines had invaded Guadalcanal and the nearby island of Tulagi in August of 1942. It was the first U.S. amphibious landing on Japanese-held islands in the Pacific War. The entire operation had been thrown together quickly, in a desperate attempt to make a stand against Japan's southward expansion toward Australia. But the U.S. Navy was stretched thin, still reeling from the loss of a significant portion of the Pacific Fleet at Pearl Harbor, less than a year earlier. The Japanese naval forces, on the other hand, were at the peak of their prowess. They held the advantage through nearby supply bases and with ships manned by highly trained and competent crews. Their deadly "Long Lance" torpedoes, destroyer-launched, had already sunk a number of Allied ships. The U.S. Navy was understandably cautious about deploying their slim forces against the overwhelming might of the Japanese navy. U.S. ships made only occasional appearances at Guadalcanal to try to support the haggard Marines in hanging on to the airfield. Two PT boat squadrons of about eight boats each had been thrown into the fray as a stopgap measure. Their mission was to harass and disrupt Japanese naval operations, and to sink enemy ships if possible. In the early days of the Pacific War, those finely tuned and well-crafted mahogany boats, with their powerful Packard engines and the offensive punch of their machine guns and torpedoes, were the only consistent U.S. naval presence in the battle for Guadalcanal. It was a daunting and hazardous challenge, and the PT boats and their crews were being pushed to the maximum. Though it was unclear at the time exactly what effect they were having, the Japanese navy could not ignore them, and their tactics were being altered accordingly. The PT boats had, indeed, sunk a couple of Japanese warships, so the enemy had to take them seriously.

The base for the PT boats was tucked into the little island of Tulagi, about 20 miles from Guadalcanal, across a body of water that would come to be known as "Iron Bottom Sound," for all the ships sunk there. Tulagi was nestled up to the larger Florida Island, to form a sheltered harbor where the PT boats could take refuge  On this particular night, February 8, 1943, Levy and Robinson had sortied out from Tulagi after dark and were headed to their assigned patrolling area on the far side of Guadalcanal. It had been a quiet night, with no sign of the Japanese. Then Levy heard, above the idling Packards on his boat, the sound of another engine. It came from a Japanese airplane out looking for PT boats. He alerted Robinson over the radio, and they throttled back and moved even closer to shore, to make it more difficult for the enemy plane to spot their wakes. The noise of the Japanese plane grew louder, but suddenly there was a startling "whump," and a geyser of water shot into the air from a bomb exploding just off the port side of Levy's boat. The concussion rocked PT 59, and a torrent of water rained down on Dave in the open cockpit and on the crew at their guns. That was close, Dave thought to himself. Another bomb exploded farther away. The Japanese pilot had either bad aim or was guessing at the PT boats' location on the dark ocean. The sound of his engine faded as he flew off into the distance. Levy and Robinson conferred on the radio and resumed their patrol. By this time the tropical sky was lightening behind the island to the east. Their patrol was over, and it was time to return back across Iron Bottom Sound to their base on Tulagi. It was nearly sunrise as they rounded Cape Esperance, the northern tip of Guadalcanal, and they angled to the right to set a course for Tulagi. But as they came around the Cape, they were confronted by an incredible scene. There were all kinds of debris, as well as men, bobbing in the ocean as far as the eye could see along the coast of Guadalcanal. The PT boats slowed their engines and idled along until they were surrounded by the floating forms of exhausted Japanese troops. These men represented what remained of the enemy force on Guadalcanal, which during the night the Japanese navy had tried to evacuate. They had only partially completed their task when it got light. Fearing deadly interference from American airplanes based at Henderson Field, the Japanese hastily curtailed evacuation efforts before they could finish loading all of their men aboard the ships. Hundreds were just abandoned, bobbing in the swells, after the Japanese navy pulled out on them. Scores of supply packages and other debris floated amidst the hordes of Japanese soldiers passively treading water and awaiting their fate. Dave Levy carefully maneuvered PT 59 amongst them, and directed members of his crew to start pulling the Japanese from the calm waters of Iron Bottom Sound. He had his submachine gun trained on the POWs as each was pulled up on deck, but none of them showed any resistance. They appeared to be totally exhausted, starving, and half sick. As tough as the Guadalcanal battle had been on the American Marines, it ultimately had been worse for the Japanese.

The early morning sun had climbed above the horizon, its rays slanting across the undulating ocean. Soon Levy had picked up seventeen Japanese soldiers, who, he figured, might just be of use to the naval intelligence section on Tulagi. Perhaps they could be interrogated to provide information of strategic importance to American plans. When he couldn't crowd any more up on the bow of the boat, he prepared to head back to Tulagi. But before gunning the engines, he noticed a Japanese flag floating next to the boat. He motioned for one of his crew to pull it from the water and give it to him. Then he shifted the telegraph handle on the cockpit's dashboard to the "full speed" position. The crewman below-deck who directly controlled the engines, known as the "motormac," opened up the throttles in response, and the PT boat leapt forward with an ear-ringing roar.

It took only about twenty minutes, running at full speed, to reach Tulagi, and as Levy rounded the reef in front of the little, green, vegetation-shrouded island, he cut the engines. Before the war, Tulagi had been the British administrative center for the rest of the Solomon Islands. A few ramshackle, thatched-roof huts and the government wharf had survived the Marine invasion, and the PT boat base was centered on the old British settlement. Levy coasted up to the government wharf, where a number of the base personnel were looking with curiosity at the wet, miserable Japanese soldiers crouched on the bow of the 59. A Marine officer approached the boat as it tied up to the wharf, and Dave turned the POWs over to him. The officer didn't seem very happy to have to deal with seventeen starving, pathetic Japanese soldiers, and he perfunctorily marched the bedraggled group inland. Dave never found out what happened to the POWs.

A few days later several of the PT boat skippers posed with Dave and the flag he had brought back. Then he sent it to his nephew back in Rochester, New York. It made the local paper, and a picture of the boy posing with a Japanese flag from the Pacific War appeared with a short article. He still has the flag to this day.

Dave's wartime experiences in the Solomon Islands would mark one of the most notable periods in his long life, which encompassed his childhood in Rochester, New York, service on PT boats in the Solomons and later the Philippines, and a post-war career as a successful lawyer. He assumed a persona in the Navy to help him get along with his fellow skippers, many of whom, unlike himself, were Ivy Leaguers and came from wealthy East Coast families. He became known as "Hogan," famous for being a deal-maker who could get things done, organize parties well-stocked with liquor and women, obtain supplies when none seemed available, and perform in the top ranks of competent PT boat skippers in those first early, desperate days of the battle for Guadalcanal.

But all of that had been far into the unimaginable future for a boy being brought up Jewish in Rochester, New York.

This book is the account of Dave "Hogan" Levy's life. It is in the format of transcriptions made from taped recollections recorded over a series of years at his vacation home in Aspen, Colorado. Each section is introduced by his co-author with a brief background that provides context for Dave's accounts, which are captured in his own dramatic words. All photos are credited to David Levy. The authors thank former fellow PT boat skippers Hugh Robinson, Huck Wood, and Jack Searles for their helpful discussions. They also acknowledge longtime colleague Walton Rawls for his expert editing of the text, and Marla Meehl for her considerable technical, editorial, and emotional support during the preparation of this book.

This book is dedicated to Mark Wertz and Hugh Robinson for what they taught Dave about operating a PT boat and about getting along in the Navy, and to Homer Facto for his expert maintenance and superb work effort on PT 59. It is also dedicated to Jerry's uncle, Al Hahn, who served in PT boat squadrons in the Mediterranean and Philippines. Although they never personally knew each other, Al was a member of the contingent of PT boat personnel that Dave shepherded across the U.S. by train in early 1945. Al also was on the *Matsonia* with Dave for the trip from California to the Philippines, and turned his boat over to Dave for decommissioning at the end of the war. It is also dedicated to Jerry's wife Marla, who has listened to countless stories from World War II veterans over the years, has traveled to numerous Pacific islands in search of old battlefields, and is a wonderfully supportive partner with Jerry in his World War II projects

# 1: GROWING UP

*Dave Levy's childhood upbringing was quite different from that of the future Ivy League PT boat skippers he would serve with in the Solomons. While Dave was dealing with the stress of being one of the only Jewish children in his school, kids like Jack Kennedy and Stilly Taylor were summering with their parents at elegant homes on the New England coast. Foreshadowing his service in PTs, Dave learned how to handle small watercraft as a child by putt-putting around parts of Long Island Sound in a small motorboat given to him by his congenial gangster step-uncle. Meanwhile, the likes of Kennedy and Taylor were priming for PTs by racing sleek sailboats in the Atlantic, off Massachusetts and Long Island. Dave scraped through college at his stepfather's alma mater, Syracuse University, while Kennedy and Taylor were over-achieving at Harvard and Princeton. Dave, the Jewish kid from Rochester, would be thrown into combat with the Ivy Leaguers, like Kennedy, Taylor, and the Searles brothers, Jack and Bob. He would have to learn how to get along with them on his own terms. He accomplished this by making a name for himself as "Hogan," and how he did this grew out of the experiences of his complicated childhood.*

*He was born on August 16, 1918, into a religious Jewish family in Rochester, New York. His life would soon be buffeted by his father's sudden death*

1

*when he was five years old. His new stepfather was also Jewish but not particularly religious. He was a driven lawyer who began a difficult lifelong relationship with his stepson shortly after he married Dave's mother in 1923.*

I had a very tough young life. My father died when I was five years old, and my mother re-married a lawyer. My natural father was very religious, but my adopted father wasn't religious at all. My adopted father was a tough guy to handle. I was a quiet kid who didn't know how to handle himself. They changed my name after my new father took me over when I was five years old. For the first time we had money, but I had been Dave Rueben and suddenly was Dave Levy. It screwed me up so much I didn't know what my name was. I was so fouled up I failed the first grade. I was a very poor student, and I didn't become a good one until I got to the seventh grade. A lot of people didn't want to talk to me. They thought I was just a screw-up.

*One of the few Jewish kids in elementary school, Rochester, 1926,*
*Dave is the second from right in back row.*

My stepfather grew up very poor, and lived in Syracuse. A teacher saw to it he went to Syracuse University. And he went to law school there, and he was in World War I. He didn't go overseas, but he was taught how to use a machine gun. When he was a kid, he made his own living and was able to get enough money together to get into law school. He would go in on the New York Central railroad, ride from Syracuse to New York City, and sell newspapers and candy along the way. He was what they called a "news butcher." If someone wanted a paper they'd yell out "hey, butch." And that's the way he had enough money to help his family and get through law school. I probably wouldn't have gotten in to Syracuse if he hadn't gone there. He grew up in Syracuse, and he moved to Rochester to practice law. I got along with him quite well. He gave me expensive fishing tackle, canoes, skis, and sent me to high caliber summer boys' camps, none of which he experienced himself when he was a kid.

However, he was generally impossible with people, and he didn't get along with my sister, but he did send her to the Eastman School of music and the University of Rochester where she graduated. And he really raised hell at a party. He'd get into talking politics. Later on he was happy to discuss politics with Jack Kennedy's father. He had a tough family. His half sister, Jane, married a gangster in New York City. His name was George De Mange. Uncle George was known as Big Frenchy De Mange. And there was probably a little Frenchy somewhere. My Aunt Jane was a beautiful woman. She danced in some shows, and she was tough as nails. And these gangsters owned two race tracks. One in Miami was named Tropical Race Track, and the other was in Massachusetts. They also owned the famous Cotton Club in New York City. They were big-time gangsters.

My mother used to get clothing sent to her for me from Uncle George, beautiful striped shirts, silk shirts, white on white, Sulka ties, and all kinds of beautiful clothing. He'd order extra stuff and send it to my mother. And I had to wear it. I looked like a junior gangster in those clothes, and I hated it! I just hated that! Later on when I finally got regular clothes, I wore button-down shirts.

3

Owney Madden was a friend of my aunt and uncle, and he was in the same gang. He was one of the big-time gangsters in the country. My parents used to send me to Long Island to stay with Aunt Jane and Uncle George. At one point Madden was in Sing Sing prison, and the day he got out of Sing Sing, I was visiting my aunt and uncle, and I went fishing with him that day on Long Island Sound. I had a great time, but I don't think that was a great start for me in life.

The gangsters of that period were tough as hell, but they were part of society. They were treated like high society. All the fine people and politicians would end up in those joints they owned. And they were accepted. Uncle George was kidnapped one time, and the gang that kidnapped him wanted to hold him up for money, and they finally gave him back and didn't kill him, but Uncle George's gang killed the ones who kidnapped him. It was a funny organization. I don't think it did me any good.

My uncle used a phony name, "Fox." I had a grandmother who had many marriages, and she was a toughy. I used to take her to the races at Saratoga. They'd give her a lot of money for the race season, and she would tell everybody, "My family is the Fox family." They were living it up pretty good. My uncle's chauffeur was George Raft. They later got him into the movies. My first wife met George Raft at the airport, and he said, "How's Aunt Jane?" After Uncle George died, Aunt Jane married a croupier out in Las Vegas, and she spent her remaining days in Las Vegas. She used to drink like a fish. She was short, so her husband, the croupier, used to put the whiskey up on the top shelf so she couldn't get to it.

The gangsters treated children and women very nicely. It was an interesting time. They gave me a boat, and I had that boat on a lake near Rochester, and I took it out on the lake all the time, and I was the hotshot kid with that boat. I drove it as fast as I could. I was driving it one day and made a quick turn and lost the motor; it went over the back. And I was no longer the hotshot kid. So I guess that gave me my nautical beginnings that stuck with me in PT boats. I loved to fish, and all those guys used to go with me as a kid and fish. I was twelve years old, and I was with those guys, and they would kid me and give me beer for lunch, and all that kind of stuff.

My Uncle George loved to play golf, and he'd come to Rochester and play at a public course and practically take the course over. He'd get hold of all the people who ran the course and give them all payoffs so he could start when he wanted to, and stop when he wanted to. He was a big shot at this public course, and he loved it. My father used to play with him. He'd bring the gang along with him, and they'd all play golf. They were known by all the other gangsters. The bootleggers in Rochester knew of Uncle George. They used to have a big 4th of July party, and they would go nuts over firecrackers. They practically blew up the area. Uncle George was famous. He knew all the politicians. He wasn't just a gangster, he was a personage, a celebrity.

They'd come down in a big Lincoln for weekends on Long Island. They'd rent a big house. My aunt Jane was in charge of everything. I met George Raft and Cab Calloway, who played for them in the Cotton Club. They had Cab Calloway and his band in Rochester at one of those movie houses, and I went down and met him. For a while they didn't let blacks come into the Cotton Club. It was high society, and they wouldn't let blacks come in. They had all kinds of black performers, but they were afraid if they let blacks come into the audience they'd cause trouble. They didn't want to lose their money.

After all his various close calls, my uncle died a natural death. Here's his obituary from *Time* Magazine, Monday, October 2, 1939:

> *Died. George Jean ("Big Frenchy") De Mange, 47, cagey onetime hoodlum, highjacker and bootlegger, latterly a millionaire Broadway restaurateur (The Club Argonaut, Park Avenue, Silver Slipper); of a heart attack; in Manhattan. As a Hudson Duster, Big Frenchy early opposed British-born Owen ("Owney") Madden's Gophers, later joined Owney in the liquor racket. In 1931 Owney scraped up $35,000 to ransom Big Frenchy when itchy-fingered Vincent Coll kidnapped him and threatened his life. Last week Owney was chief mourner at Big Frenchy's funeral, complete with six cars dripping with flowers.*

I was never proud of my gangster connections, but that certainly wisened me up to a lot of stuff that was going on. It probably helped me in some ways. I became a real operator later, and maybe watching my uncle and his friends operate gave me some ideas on how to do it. But it probably hindered me in some ways as a lawyer. A lot of people didn't respect those kinds of connections. But I did have a problem, and it wasn't my fault. Here I am going to high school wearing Sulka ties, and in those days they cost 100 bucks. I was dressed like a junior gangster, and I didn't like being dressed that way. That gangster stuff may have affected me, but not as much as you'd think. I never talked about this stuff in college, and it sort of made me different from the other kids.

When I was in high school I played guard on the football team, and I was a Democrat, while everybody who lived in my neighborhood were wealthy Republicans. The only people who were Democrats were the teachers, so the teachers were real nice to me. Every Friday we'd give speeches, and I'd get up and give speeches about the Democrats, and I'd tell the class about the "three C's," the Civilian Conservation Corps (CCC). I met some of those people in Syracuse, and they were rebuilding parks, and things like that. A lot of those guys were boxers, and they were from the inner cities, working for the CCC, and it was very foreign for them to be out in the country. One of them became a state Supreme

Court judge in Rochester. I used to see him a lot. He was an Italian guy. I used to give a speech on that. I used to like that sort of thing.

*High school football team, 1935. Dave is third from right in front row.*

One of my best friends was another kid in Rochester, named Rod Smith. Everyone called him "Smitty." Starting when we were only about twelve or thirteen, every summer his parents would drop us off in Canada with my canoe, and we'd be on our own fishing for a couple of weeks, and then my parents would pick us up. We met a young French Canadian guy who was kind of like our guide, and he'd join us every summer. Our friends' parents thought our parents didn't like us and wanted to get rid of us. But what it did was teach us how to operate on our own, and we learned how to fish, and I've fished for the rest of my life. We did things like figuring out how to cook beans. We'd put the beans in an iron pot in a hole, then cover the pot up with sand and build a fire on the sand and let it burn overnight. Then the next day we'd have great baked beans.

Another real close childhood friend of mine was John Jack, and he remains a good friend to this day. He has the wonderful characteristic that he never speaks badly about anyone. He was also in the navy during the war, and he was a supply officer at various big supply depots, including one in Alaska. He was quite successful in business and he has a very nice family.

During the summers when I was a teenager, I was a life guard at a big camp site in the Adirondacks, at a huge lake. I did that for three summers, and I learned to handle girls there. There were a lot of girls from Montreal. I ran that beach. It was interesting. I took care of a couple of girls that were drowning. I pulled them out. In college I did the same thing. One summer I climbed the highest mountain in the Adirondacks. It was called Mount Marcy, and up there was an area called the Floudlands, the source of the Hudson River. It was kind of a marshy area, and there were a lot of springs and ponds. At that altitude the water was cold, and there was excellent fishing. They had trout, and they grew beautifully in those ponds. I'd carry a canoe up that mountain to the Floudlands, and I had a hell of a time getting it up there. My canoe was wood and weighed about ninety pounds, but it was worth it for the great fishing.

I grew up in a neighborhood with very wealthy people who didn't like Jews. And the mothers wouldn't let me go out with their daughters, so I never had anything to do with girls when I was younger. That's probably why I was so active later on. I went to Syracuse University and had the same problems there. At that time, Jews were not well-accepted at Syracuse. In those days, Eastman Kodak Company in Rochester had built subdivisions, and in the deeds they didn't permit Jews to live in the subdivisions. After the war the G.I. Bill ended that bad period, because then everyone went to college, and it changed everything. But it was tough for me to handle as a kid, and tough for me in the service until I got known. After I got known, I made it all right. But I tried to do a lot to make people like me. I gave parties, I did everything. It was a very big part of my life. It was a reason I became an operator in the Navy. I got accepted, and I was well-accepted.

I graduated from high school and went to Syracuse University. My undergraduate degree was in political science, and they had a good political science course there. But I was a loud, terrible student, with a bad, kind of aimless, attitude. I used to get disgusted and walk on the railroad tracks out of town. I graduated college June 1st of 1941, and I knew everybody was waiting for me in the service. Some people were avoiding the service by taking engineering. But I figured I'd get into the service, so I was trying to work out what would be the best deal I could make, and I was thinking of everything.

# 2:  GETTING INTO PT BOATS

*For many young men graduating from college in the spring of 1941, it was clear that war was on the horizon, and a number of them made a proactive decision to join the military. Dave was one of them. Although he didn't have any inkling of what PT boats were all about, he instinctively knew that getting into the Navy's smaller vessels was the best thing for someone like him. With a fundamentally rebellious nature, he realized he just wouldn't get along too well with the strict Navy regulations enforced on large ships. His first thought was of destroyers, but he ended up more or less by chance in PT boats. When the war started, the sons of wealthy families maneuvered mightily, using their connections, to get assigned to those small boats. PTs were the hot rods of the Navy, and they appealed greatly to young college graduates fresh out of officer training. They knew there was no quicker route to commanding a U.S. Navy ship when just a newly minted lieutenant.*

The first thing I did after graduating from Syracuse was to volunteer for the Marine Corps Officer's Training School. I didn't know how safe it was or anything, and I had no idea what the Marines were. So a colonel from the Marines, an Annapolis graduate, came to Syracuse to look us over and see who would qualify. And he put us in the order of the way he wanted to choose us, and I was number five. There were four ahead of me, and they were all football players and tough, physically fit guys. Two of them I knew from freshmen football, both were guards, and I was a guard. One would block you just enough so that your fingertips could not touch the runner who had the ball. The other didn't stop blocking you until he would have you outside the stadium.

There was a lot of feeling against Jewish kids in the college, and I thought that's why he made me number five, and I was mad as hell at him. It turned out that those four guys ahead of me all went to Guadalcanal, and all of them ended up being killed in the Pacific.

Then I decided, well, my next bet is the Navy. I couldn't get into the Officer's Training School in the Navy because they required math, and I had no math in college. So I got them to commit that if I took a summer course in math they'd take me into the program. I went to the University of Rochester and took a summer course in math, and then I got in. So, I was in the Navy in September of 1941.

They ran me through an officers training course to turn me into a "90-day wonder." We were at Tower Hall at Northwestern University, where they had the water tower. The Chicago football team, the Bears, was practicing in an armory, and I used to go and watch them. On December 7th my roommate and I went out for a walk in Chicago. We were finishing up our 90-day wonder course, and we were out walking. I took a picture of him at the edge of the lake. We found out about the Pearl Harbor attack after we got back from our walk. I wasn't sure where I was going to end up. In fact they once talked about sending us to Alaska.

I decided that I wanted to get into small boats. I was looking for destroyers, since I heard that the bigger ships were very tough and needed a little etiquette and social things and all that kind of baloney, and you had to dress up and all of that. So I volunteered for the torpedo school at Newport, Rhode Island, figuring destroyers had torpedoes on them and that would get me into destroyers. I went to torpedo school with no idea of getting into PT boats, but they asked for volunteers for PT boats from the torpedo school because they could use our knowledge. And that's how I got into PT boats. I didn't know what the hell I was getting into. I had no idea.

*Dave as a freshly minted ensign in the United States Navy, Christmas, 1941. Photo was taken at the end of his "90 day wonder" training program at Northwestern University.*

Then it turned out that all the hotshot kids were trying to get on PT boats. But that wasn't my angle. I didn't use my background or anything else. I just happened to be at the right place at the right time, or the wrong place. A lot of the guys who volunteered for PT boats had sailing experience. There seemed to be a lot of Ivy Leaguers. There were also a lot of football players. They had enough football players to have a team at Newport. They played Holy Cross and Harvard and teams like that. I was the first class out of there, and I was twenty-one years old.

I quickly got very good at navigating, and I don't really know why. But I learned how to navigate in a hurry, and I had a good feeling for what I was to use it for. So they took me right out of training, and gave me a boat alone, with no other officers. Usually there were two or three officers on a boat. But they trusted me because I was able to find my way. And, you know, you didn't have many chances to get out on a boat. Usually you went out with a senior officer, and he told you to go around to various places.

But I was very poor at some other things. I couldn't shoot a .45 caliber pistol. As a kid, I hated guns. I don't know why, but I couldn't shoot that damn pistol. Anyway, they were horrible. They have a terrible kick to them, and I was always anticipating the kick, so I'd pull up and couldn't qualify. But I qualified by getting hold of a spare target and punching in "bullet holes" with a pencil. But I was able to use the light submachine guns that we had. The Marines loved those submachine guns. They stole a few from us in the Solomons. We used them when we had guys in the water, picking up Japs, and all that. But I was able to use it because it was easy, and it didn't kick. You could do anything you wanted with it. But I went through the whole war without shooting the .45 they gave me, because if I'd shot it I'd have had to take it apart and clean it; so I never shot it.

I think what really helped me in training at Newport was that I had just graduated from college and was absorbing stuff very quickly. The older people that came into the Navy found it impossible, because it was coming too fast for them. When you are a senior in college, you really absorb stuff and know how to take tests. I mean, the knowledge of knowing how to take a test was more important than the knowledge that you know. The guys who just got out of college were prime. Those that came in three and four years after graduating had a hell of a time.

We had some really fine young regular Navy officers who had been in PT boats. Some of these people had been with the PT boat squadron out in Hawaii, and that was the first squadron. And we had the same kind of boats that they had. As soon as we got involved with them in training, we learned a hell of a lot. But we learned everything that we really knew about PT boats in Panama. We were in Panama for a couple of months. And the guys that had been in longer took us out and taught us everything. And they were the best. And the following squadrons never had that kind of thing. They only had one guy who knew what was going on, but we got mixed in with a whole squadron of those guys, and they were good.

It was unpleasant when we would cruise around in the ocean off the east coast where there were strong currents, the Gulf Stream. We'd go through it, and we'd be in it for quite a while, and the waves were in the form of mountains, and you couldn't predict where they would come up, and you had one hell of a time with a PT boat in that current.

We had some dumb stuff happen during training. I saw a PT boat sink one of our big Merchant Marine ships at Narragansett Harbor, by mistake. We were doing a night patrol, a submarine patrol, off in the Atlantic, and this was when we first started. It was only for practice. In a PT boat, the torpedoes are in tubes, and you blow them out with gunpowder. Well, this guy armed the torpedoes in the bay by turning the key. To fire a torpedo, there was a key you'd turn and then you press a button. Well, somebody leaned against the keys and the buttons, and two torpedoes went down Narragansett Bay, about four miles, and hit this Merchant Marine ship. Ohhh, geez! And nothing was ever said about it.

We were at Nantucket Harbor just playing around, and we thought we'd give the girls a treat by showing them a couple of explosions. So, we went on around, and we dropped a couple of depth charges. Well, the depth charges were set for 60 feet, and there was 25 feet of water. So, these armed depth charges just sat in the harbor. They're probably still there. Now, that's the kind of dumb thing that was happening all the time.

I did a lot of stupid things with women. I was really a stupid ass. I had a bad reputation. In Newport, Rhode Island, when I was first there, there was a fellow who owned a bar, a Mr. Hogan. And I went out with Mrs. Hogan. And all the guys were saying "Hogan, they're after you, they're after you." And they called me Hogan. And that lasted during the whole war. A lot of my friends looked me up in the service, and they'd say, "Is Mr. Levy here?" They'd say, "Well, we don't have a Mr. Levy, but we have a Mr. Hogan." It stayed with me. I couldn't get rid of it. When John Kennedy met me in Rochester after the war, he said to my wife, "Ohhh, Mrs. Hogan. How are you?" My wife was OK with that since she knew the story.

I don't know what it was about the PT boats that appealed to all these Ivy League guys. Most of these guys had gotten in early. Jack Searles and his brother Bob were a couple of years older than us. But the rest of them, they graduated about the same time I did. They thought PT boats were fun and they were small and you could be the skipper, the same reasons I suppose I volunteered, because I didn't want to get on a big ship and have all the regulations of a big ship. I mean, you know, on a big ship you've got to get up on time, you've got to get dressed, you've got to be sparkling clean, you've got to have your shoes shining, and that wasn't me. And you always have a dumber guy ahead of you, but you had so many more of them on a big ship.

When I got into PT boats, there were a lot of hotshots, six or seven from Princeton, and they all stuck together, and they made it easy for each other, and they didn't have anything to do with me. I made it because I was able to learn how to operate, and they respected me for how I could operate. They initially weren't friendly with me. They were all from major schools, and Syracuse wasn't considered a major school. If they didn't know what I was doing, they didn't have any time for me.

Mark Wertz had been in the Navy in PT boats with that group in the Philippines, and he helped me, and he was wonderful. He was probably one of my best friends in PT boats. He got me into the group, and he taught me how to operate the boat. It was quite difficult to learn how to operate one of those boats. There was no direct drive, you had to telegraph everything. So if you were going to back up, you had to set the telegraph lever on the dashboard in the cockpit to the reverse setting. Then that setting was seen on a similar telegraph in the engine room by the motor machinist mate or "motormac" down there on the engines, and then the motormac engaged the engines and the boat went back, and that made a time difference from when you signaled you wanted to go back to the time you actually went back. Same thing with going forward. It was very difficult to know how much power to use around docks and things. So I had good luck, and Wertz taught me all the tricks he knew. He had a wife and three kids, was older, a bridge engineer. He went to Lehigh, and knew technical stuff very well. When we were in Newport, he'd invite me to go to his house.

Just before the war I took friends to the Cotton Club, some guys from Melville, Long Island, in PT training. They couldn't believe how they treated us because my Uncle George, "Big Frenchy," owned the place. We had an "in." They enjoyed it. Later on, I was at my Aunt Jane's apartment on Fifth Avenue in New York City, and remember she went by "Jane Fox," and I got a telegram that my leave was canceled and I was on my way to the Pacific. Our boats had gotten to Norfolk, so I left from Norfolk. They had the boats loaded with guys for a training operation, and we took the boats all the way through the Caribbean, and we ended up in Panama. The water was beautiful in the Caribbean. We stopped a few times; one stop was at Jamaica. We drove them all the way from Norfolk to Panama.

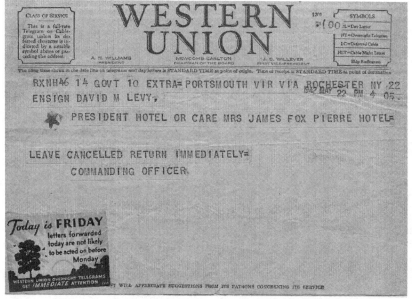

*Dave was on leave visiting his Aunt Jane, wife of George "Big Frenchy" De Mange, in New York City in May, 1942, when he got this telegram ordering him to report to duty to take PT 59 to Panama and eventually to the South Pacific. His Aunt Jane and Uncle George went by the name "Mr. and Mrs. James Fox", so the telegram was addressed to Dave in care of "Mrs. James Fox".*

# 3: PANAMA

*The newly trained PT boat squadrons were first sent to Panama in 1942. They were to guard the canal, and perhaps be deployed up and down the Central and South American coasts on anti-submarine duty. While in Panama the new skippers and crews continued to learn about PT boats. Some of their teachers were combat veterans from the PT boat squadrons in the Philippines, or experienced PT boat operators from the squadrons that had been in Hawaii. Young skippers like Dave also had to learn how to handle the enlisted men on their boats. This was not too straightforward for recent college graduates and inexperienced naval officers. The months spent in Panama were also filled with shore leave and other adventures. But the time was soon to come when the men would be shipped to the Pacific for some of the first island combat with the Japanese.*

I had a bunch of Navy professional sailors on my boat—old-timers—and they didn't take to us very well, young officers like me telling them what to do. These were the ones who were already in the service before they opened up training at Newport. I later had some trouble with them because they thought I was taking too many chances. There were two of these enlisted guys, a machinist mate and one who helped navigate, and they had been in the Navy for quite a number of years. And one of them absolutely hated me for being a 90-day wonder, and being in charge of him. He got drunk on torpedo alcohol one day, and he was in the boat when I reported to it. And the crew said there's a guy down below decks in the crew quarters, and he's drunk. I went down there, and he had a gun; he was waving a .45 around. And right then and there I learned what being an officer in the Navy was like. He was showing me that he was the boss, and you just can't have that. So he was waving the gun around, and I just took it away from him, just took it away. When you're twenty-one years old, you're dumb. Finally he recognized there'd be plenty of goddamn trouble if he didn't give me the gun. Then he turned out to be all right, but not on my boat. I got rid of him.

I had to figure out how to handle people when I got into small boats, and this was something I had to learn. I'd never had to manage or organize or order people around before, and when you are in charge of a PT boat you need to be able to handle the crew. I learned that if you get too close to them and then you're tough on them, you end up with nothing. In the beginning all the PT boat crews were picked specially, but they were still unknowns until you got them together on a boat. The guys on my crew all turned out pretty good.

I never applied the Navy regulations to anyone. So if they were drinking torpedo alcohol on my boat, I never turned them in. I never turned in the guy who was drunk and threatened me with the gun. The whole experience was a real lesson in how to treat people when you're that close to them. You had to let them get away with a certain amount, and you couldn't be too tough. But sometimes I had to be tough if I needed them.

One of the crew drew a little cartoon they gave to me. It was titled "Hogan being mad." It was a drawing of me kind of looking like an angry animal. So, yes, I guess every now and then I was tough on them. But they knew that was part of my job, and they recognized that and gave me that little drawing. I still have it.

But even after saying all that, the key for me was a guy on my crew named Homer Facto. He was a little older, and I'd let him handle the young guys, and he was great with them.

So the torpedo alcohol was something we had to deal with. I'd let them drink if we weren't going out, but if we had a night patrol coming up, I'd stop the drinking in the afternoon so they were ready by evening for the patrol. I'd tell Homer, and he'd get them ready. The crew respected me, and I didn't ever really have any trouble.

You couldn't make guys do things according to the book. You had to let them go and do what they wanted to do and hope they did the right thing. You couldn't really direct them either. If you put them on a gun, you couldn't direct them on the gun. It was very loose. A guy like Facto was a wonderful guy to have because he kept track of some of these guys who weren't so good at what they were doing.

My crew was a bunch of kids, really. They did crazy things, playing, and sometimes not to your benefit. They'd include me sometimes, but I'd have to make sure I wasn't too much of a buddy to them. On our way to Panama we stopped in Jamaica. The crew had been to a local whorehouse, and they saw something that was so amazing to them they had to show it to me. So they took me to this place, and in this room there was a girl who was crouched up on a sink in the corner cleaning herself with the faucets turned so they pointed up. The guys thought this was one of the most amazing gymnastic feats they'd ever seen. She was agile, like a monkey, and they thought this was so interesting I just had to see it. So I appreciated that they included me. I had to be careful to keep a little distance, but still relate to them.

21

There were other times these kids behaved like they were about fifteen years old. And when you think of it, they'd come right into the Navy from home, and they had just been under the control of their parents right before that, so I was careful not to be too tough on them. If you were, you had nothing. A PT boat was very different from a big Navy ship. I didn't enforce any Navy regulations. We all dressed any way we wanted to that was comfortable. You'd never get away with that on a big Navy ship.

I never wore a Navy uniform on my boat. I'd brought along six pairs of Navy whites onto the boat, and never wore them. They finally turned green in the tropical humidity, and I threw them overboard. I also had a sword. Now what you'd do with a sword in the Navy I don't know, but it rusted and I threw it overboard too.

I found out that the farm kids on my crew tended to be good shots—they were good with shooting the guns. Then they'd have to clean their guns, but I never gave them orders to do that. I got Homer to get them to clean up.

We actually had better PT boats at the beginning of the war than at the end. Later on they loaded them down with too many guns, and the extra weight didn't make them operate as well. I thought the Elco boats were engineered the best. The Higgins and Huckins weren't as good. They were heavier and went fifteen knots slower. The Elco was built light. The hull was made of planks of wood cut into long pieces and laminated together. There were two layers of wood at an angle, screwed to the frame with hundreds of screws, and there was Egyptian cotton between the two layers, and it was glued together with marine glue. This made repairs difficult, because the wood would splinter if it was hit. Then, later, the wood would delaminate, and the movement of the boat would make it come off the frame. At the end of the war when we were burning the surplus PT boats, a lot of them had this problem, the hulls had started to come off the frames.

I was assigned to PT 59, and it never got seriously damaged. I took the 59 to the Caribbean, and it was in the last group of 77-foot Elco boats. Then they went to 80 feet, and those boats got overloaded and didn't operate as well as the 77-footers.

Robert Montgomery, the actor, wanted to get into PT boats. He was with me in officers training. He was a little older and acted dumb. By that I mean he wasn't stupid intelligence-wise, but he just didn't do very well in training. I think that's because the rest of us had all just come out of college, and we were used to studying and knew how to take exams. Montgomery was older and had been out of school for a while, and he had a hell of a time passing the exams. He was with us in Panama, and he lived like a king. He'd go with us into a restaurant and he'd gather up the B-girls and buy them whiskey. He later got into the PT boat movie *They Were Expendable.*

There were a lot of whores in Panama, but they were pretty high class. They were Americans, and they would come down from the States and stay a couple of weeks in Panama and make a lot of money and leave again. They were tough as nails. There were also local native whores who would come around carrying their babies. That was really terrible. Panama was a rough place.

I started there to become famous for being an operator. The men thought that maybe because I was Jewish I could do anything. They had some idea that Jewish people could make good business deals. And I lived up to that reputation. When I was in Panama they sent me out to buy wristwatches for every officer. I was able to make deals for almost anything. I could go into a jewelry story and give them some kind of Navy certificate and get anything I wanted. We didn't have a lot of things on the boat, so I got stuff for the crew. I was able to get a Navy certificate saying that I could buy things—that I bought them for the Navy. I was able to supply those guys with a lot of things they could use. To them I was "Hogan." I could operate. I became a personage because I did all this stuff, and I was accepted by all these hotshots because of this. And it changed me.

# 4: TULAGI AND GUADALCANAL

*American Marines landed in the Solomon Islands in August of 1942. It was an operation hastily planned to stop the Japanese from completing an airstrip they had started to build on Guadalcanal. Once established, a Japanese air base in the Solomons would be close enough to support an invasion of Australia. But the American Navy was ill-equipped at the time to support the Marine force in their battle with the Japanese. Still struggling to recover from the devastating blow received at Pearl Harbor, the Navy was reluctant to risk its remaining ships in any kind of sustained confrontation. After landing the Marines with but a portion of the supplies they would need, the U.S. Navy made only periodic appearances off the coast of Guadalcanal as the Marines battled to retain control of the airstrip they'd captured, and to keep from being driven back into the ocean. Every conceivable resource had to be brought to bear, and the PT boats in Panama were shipped northwestward to confront the Japanese navy. A ramshackle, improvised PT boat base was quickly built on Tulagi Island, across Iron Bottom Sound from Guadalcanal. The American air presence on the Guadalcanal airstrip kept the Japanese navy from boldly attacking by day, but almost nightly visits by what Americans called the "Tokyo Express" were mostly uncontested. These were warships that shelled the American airstrip and Japanese transports that supplied their troops on the island. The PT boats were brought in to do something about* that. Though far out-gunned and relying on faulty and aged torpedoes (some of them from World War I), the PT boats were the only consistent U.S. naval presence for those last few months of 1942, right up until the Japanese evacuated their troops from Guadalcanal in defeat in early February, 1943. Joe Foss, a Marine pilot and Medal of Honor winner for his actions during the battle for Guadalcanal, summed up the American effort against the Japanese this way: "Those untested, under-equipped, and seemingly unqualified young men didn't just beat back the attacking force, they wiped it out, handing the Japanese Army its first defeat in a thousand years." The PT boats played a key role in that victory. They confronted the superior naval forces of Japan, and even sank a few ships. They harassed the Japanese, who had to take them seriously or risk getting their ships shot up or occasionally sunk. The PT boats were the Navy that showed up at Guadalcanal, and proved crucial to the first American triumph in the island battles of the Pacific.

We shipped out from Panama and headed across the Pacific on a transport with our PT boats stowed onboard. This was fall, 1942, and the Marines had just invaded Guadalcanal and Tulagi in the Solomons. We unloaded the boats at Noumea, New Caledonia, and then we were towed up to the Solomons, two PT boats behind each destroyer. When they towed us to Guadalcanal, I was in the boat for the couple of days it took. We had to steer our boats to keep them from hitting each other. There was a big, long cable, and it would've destroyed the damn boat if you hadn't been steering. And that was supposed to be from Noumea all the way up to Guadalcanal. It was lousy steering. You couldn't really control it. The boat would start going from side to side, and sometimes we'd almost get sideways. So maybe a hundred miles or so before we got to Guadalcanal, those destroyers said they were dropping us off, right there in the middle of the ocean. They didn't want to get any closer to Guadalcanal. I was glad to get unhooked. Getting towed was hard on the boat and hard on the people. So we drove the boats the rest of the way up to Guadalcanal and Tulagi.

I'd never heard of Guadalcanal. Nobody was talking about it much then. You know, we spent maybe five weeks at sea from Panama to New Caledonia, and we didn't know a thing then. When we got to Guadalcanal, we didn't go ashore. We just immediately went over to Tulagi, which is across Iron Bottom Bay from Guadalcanal.

Tulagi was a fairly small island, and the Marines had invaded and cleared it out before we got there. So Tulagi is where they set up our PT boat base. They let us off, and then they left. We didn't see the Navy after that for a long time. Those destroyers turned around, and they were soooo glad to get the hell out of there. And we're sitting there on this little island, and it's very quiet. My idea of what war was like was the movie *All Quiet on the Western Front*. I'd seen it as a kid at least sixteen times, and that was my idea of what war was. The movie was about trench warfare, and I thought war was fought in trenches. No matter what they taught me, no matter what I read, I was looking for that kind of a war. PT boats were quite a bit different from the movies. So I'm standing there, in my PT boat, looking across the bay over at Guadalcanal, and I thought, "God, there's nothing going on here. I can't believe it." Of course things started happening pretty soon, but it wasn't trench warfare.

I got to the Solomons in November of 1942 with Squadron 2. We called it "Ron 2," and we initially had eight boats. I think the Marines invaded Guadalcanal in August, so I was there close to the beginning. Another PT boat squadron, Ron 3, got there about a month ahead of us with eight boats, and they were pretty beat up when we got there, and they had lost boats. As a result of losing boats, we had more crews than boats, so we went on patrol every other night, and I shared my boat with another crew. Luckily my boat, the 59, stayed together all the time, but we were really there on a shoestring. We just got barely enough fuel to keep going, and we didn't get anything much to eat. We ate Spam for two and a half months. Nothing came in. There were supposed to be twelve boats in a squadron, but we had less than that because of the losses. Those first two squadrons were the only U.S. Navy there in the Solomons until, maybe, December or so.

*PT 59 with Dave at the helm, between Tulagi and Guadalcanal, late 1942.*

*PT 59 with Dave at the helm, cruising into Tulagi harbor, late 1942.*

When we first got to Tulagi, the PT boat tender *Jamestown* was there, and I lived on the *Jamestown*, and it was comfortable. It was a big motor yacht they'd converted to a tender, and they used it to maintain the operation. I lived there and lived on the beach too. We were sleeping a hell of a lot during the days because we were going out every other night.

When we got to Tulagi we were the only ones there. The Japanese would come around every so often to bomb us. When we had air raids, we learned very quickly that if you shoot back you give away your position. There was also some danger of getting hit by the falling shrapnel from the other ships shooting at the Japanese planes. But the real problem was the stupid people who would shoot anyhow and light up the sky over them. We only shot when the Japs were close, and then we had to. We kept Tulagi fairly clean from other aircraft. At the end of my stay there, we were getting a lot of new ships, and those new ships would light up the sky when enemy planes came over. You know, there were so many dumb things done without any orders.

*This Japanese zero was shot down over Tulagi during an air raid, December, 1942.*

There was no official position about what to do if we ever got captured, and they didn't tell us a hell of a lot. So they didn't tell us what to do in that situation. It was surprising that there were no orders on anything. I was aware that the Japs were tough, and it would be foolish to just give yourself up to them, because you wouldn't live very long. I didn't know enough about the area to know where to go to evade the Japs, and we had no orders on where to go, and we didn't even know what direction to go. I don't think you could have escaped the Japs. If we got caught, that would have been the end. It could have been that they weren't that mean and nasty, but they didn't have any facilities to keep or take care of prisoners, and they didn't want to spend the time or the men to look after prisoners. And it was the same for the Marines. They were doing the same thing. We didn't have the men to look after prisoners. But the Japs were bad. They realized they would get shot or we would get shot.

I should have fished, but I didn't. I didn't pay any attention. I just ate what they gave me, and it was awful stuff, mostly Spam. I hated Spam. Some people liked it. There was a distinction between the officers and the non-officers. The non-officers all ate on the boats. And I never ate on the boats. I always ate in the mess hall on shore or on the *Jamestown*. They gave the officers a break. We had better sleeping accommodations. There were a lot of people on the boats, which were small, and it was uncomfortable. They were hot. I never slept in the boats regularly. When I was out on patrol and everything was clear, I went to sleep.

We didn't have much in the way of briefings. They were quiet about having broken the Japanese code, and we thought we were getting this information from coast watchers. But they'd tell us where we'd be going, and what to look for. Sometimes someone would come to the boat and tell us where we'd be going, and we'd pass the word. We'd talk about it, and they'd get us the information, but it wasn't very thorough, and it didn't help a hell of a lot.

We'd go in to the government wharf at Sesapi on Tulagi in the evening when we were ready to go out, and first we'd have a briefing, and they'd say there were going to be so many ships coming at us: they're going to let off troops or they're going to take on troops or they're going to do this and they're going to do that and you go to this position to intercept. But, you know, most of the time it wouldn't work like clockwork. To get to those places at night, in absolute darkness, you know, you're playing blind man's buff. And sometimes you'd get there, and sometimes you wouldn't. We never paid much attention to how they were getting the information, except on that last night when the Japs left Guadalcanal. I could tell then they knew exactly everything. But, up until then, I didn't know how they were getting it. I thought maybe they were getting it from coast watchers. But the coast watchers really only confirmed what the Japs did. And the coast watchers couldn't put out signals all the time. The Japs were just too close to them. But that was a very interesting part of the war, to me.

So the skippers got together for briefings in a hut on shore at Sesapi, near the old government wharf. There usually wasn't much to talk about, just where the boats going out that night would patrol, and maybe what we could expect, but most of the time we just went out on patrol and dealt with whatever happened. We were looking to disrupt the Japanese ships attacking Guadalcanal, or unloading supplies for the Japanese troops, and we'd just go to an assigned area to patrol over by Guadalcanal and look for the Japanese ships.

*Scene at the Sesapi dock at the PT boat base on Tulagi after an overnight patrol, December, 1942.*

*PT boats docked at the PT boat base at Sesapi, Tulagi, December, 1942.*

*PT boats docked at the PT boat base at Sesapi, Tulagi, December, 1942.*

*Machine shop at PT boat base, Tulagi, December, 1942.*

*A shell fired from a Japanese destroyer went right through the bow of this Ron 3
PT boat docked at Tulagi after an overnight patrol, late 1942.*

I was the only one who went out with one officer aboard. All the rest had two officers aboard. I always felt I would come out OK on the 59, and because of that I was hesitant to go out on other boats. My whole crew felt that way. One evening the call came out for another boat to go out on patrol. The 59 had already gone out with another crew, and I was standing there next to PT 37 with Jim Kelly, and one of us had to take out the 37. We cut cards to see who would go. Kelly cut a king, and I cut an ace, so Kelly went out. That night PT 37 was destroyed by shellfire. Only Eldon Jenter survived from that crew, and Jim Kelly was killed.

The Japanese had a lot of planes that weren't great fighting aircraft. On their cruisers they had seaplanes, but they had heavy bombs on them and were fairly slow, so you could usually get away. We had several air raids while we were at Tulagi. They'd drop a bunch of bombs but didn't really hit anything, and they didn't come in to strafe, they didn't come in that low. We'd hide the boats under brush during the day. We never moved the boats during an air raid if they were already hidden, but we'd man the guns and shoot at the planes.

There was a small New Zealand ship, a corvette, that was with us a lot of the time. The crew were wonderful people to deal with, and they had good whiskey. They were a lot of fun. And they got sunk on one of the last days the Japs came down. We lost a hell of a lot of people on those ships, and we just never saw them again.

We got shot at from shore on Guadalcanal quite a bit. That's why one guy left my boat, because he thought I was taking too many chances. We were close to shore at night and couldn't see what was going on, and the Japanese started firing pretty-large-caliber guns at us, and thank God they didn't hit us. And I got shot at like that twice. I was shot at a lot of times with small-caliber guns. But when you're shot at and you're missed, you don't pay that much attention to it. I never had anyone injured and never lost anybody.

There was one guy who was on my boat for a little while, Red Reilly we called him. He was a blond, Irish kid, and he was my Exec for a few weeks. And then he went to another boat, and he was killed on that boat almost immediately, and I knew him quite well. He was a nice guy. It was one of those things where they fired a torpedo and tried to get away too quickly, and they were blown up. I think all the guys on the boat were killed. This was something we talked about a lot, whether it was better to gun it and get the hell away as fast as possible after firing your torpedoes, but then your wake lights up with foam and phosphorescence and the Japs can see you; or to leave slowly and don't create much of a wake. It's more nerve-wracking going away slowly, but that's what I always did, because I kept hearing about boats going away fast and getting shot up because it was easier for the Japs to see them.

*Raymond "Red" Reilly on PT 59, Tulagi, early 1943. Shortly after this photo was taken, Reilly transferred to another boat and was killed in action.*

When we were patrolling we saw a lot of gunfire, and out there in the dark we didn't know exactly where it was coming from. What we determined, after a very short time, was that if the Japs could see you you'd better watch out, so we had smoke generators on our boats, but I don't think they really did a hell of a lot of good. Some people in PT boats made stupid moves, and then that was the end of them. Like if your boat was dead in the water, the Japs couldn't see you. If you were going fast, you made a huge wake and you were singing. But you made one hell of a good target. We actually usually moved around only at 10-15 knots, just so we wouldn't be seen.

There was another guy, I later learned, from the Boston area. He was on a supply ship and didn't like it and wanted to get into PT boats. So he used his father's pull to get into PT boats. They sent him to Tulagi to see what it was like. He went out on one mission, and on that mission he got killed. He didn't have any reason to go on that boat except to find out what it was like.

I never realized when we were there that we were the only thing between the Japs and New Zealand and Australia. I never had a feeling for the overall strategy, and I never had a feeling for why we ate Spam for two months. You know, the Navy was having plenty of problems, and they weren't helping us very much, and we were the only thing left there, just us and the Marines on the shore on Guadalcanal. I kept seeing the Marines, but I didn't really realize how important the airfield on Guadalcanal was. We just didn't know how important Guadalcanal was. Had we lost that airfield it would've been all over, and the Japs would've been on their way to Australia.

We also didn't know how desperate the situation was, and how close we came to losing the battle for Guadalcanal. We knew we weren't getting enough food, ammunition, or supplies, and we knew our Navy wasn't sticking around much, but we didn't know how bad things really were.

We were sent there under some of the worst conditions any American fighting force ever endured. It was all on a shoestring, and there was no real ability to keep us supplied or supported. These were really difficult conditions, but at the time we didn't realize how bad it really was. The high command never told us what was going on, and we never talked about it much. We had our assignment, and we went out at night and went after the Japanese warships and didn't ask any questions. It's only recently that I've begun to wonder what would have happened if we had lost Guadalcanal. We'd have been stuck there, and we'd have probably been captured or killed by the Japanese. We didn't have enough fuel to get us back to the American base at Noumea on New Caledonia. It would have been just as difficult for our Navy to evacuate the Marines and us as it was for the Japanese to evacuate their troops from Guadalcanal after they lost, and they ended up leaving a lot of their people. They couldn't get them all out. But we weren't thinking about that. We were just going a day at a time, and doing our job, and not asking any questions.

One of the nights I had off, Jack Searles took my boat out (December 9, 1942). He was in Squadron 3. We had broken the Jap code, and our intelligence people had figured out exactly where and when a Japanese general was coming into Guadalcanal on a submarine. So Searles was sent out there with my boat. The submarine came up at that location at that time, and they fired their torpedoes at it and blew it up. This was one of the real notable things that happened there in the early going. Searles got the Navy Cross for that.

We always saw planes flying around during the day, ours and theirs. A lot of planes went down off the airfield on Guadalcanal. In fact, we were sent to pick up our pilots when they went down. Some of them ran out of fuel if they went too far north. They went to Bougainville to bomb, and then coming back they would run out of fuel and would try to crash land on the reefs, particularly the torpedo planes. I saw a whole squadron go down within, oh, maybe 50-60 miles of the field on

Guadalcanal. We were out there in our boats and saw them going in, and then we heard over the radio they were going down. They were just getting lower and lower, and pretty soon they were in the water. I picked up a few of the pilots who survived. There was so much of that, so many mistakes. In the service we call them "fuck ups."

In the Solomons, our PT boats were no match for a Japanese destroyer. If the Japs could see you, you were hit. They got you. The Japanese navy and army were experts. We didn't realize it at first, but we did realize it after awhile. They had been at war for six years, and they were good. I mean their destroyers just raised hell with our whole Navy. They sank our cruisers one after another. And their torpedoes were good. They worked. And we were using World War I torpedoes that weren't very great. So for a while our PT boats were the only thing there. Every night we'd go out, and we'd report some Jap ship was hit or sunk, but it wasn't necessarily so.

One night, some admiral came through. We were all out in our PT boats, and he put out the word over the radio, "Get the hell out of the way, I'm coming through." He didn't want the PT boats around. He had cruisers with him, and four of our cruisers got it that night. You couldn't ever really know what was going on, and that was the case that night. You know, it was just confusion. You don't really know what the hell is going on. And I'm sure that admiral didn't know what the hell was going on either.

One of the cruisers, the *Northampton*, was sunk. They sent us out the next morning to look for survivors. I picked up three sailors on my boat, and they were really glad we found them. A couple of the other boats picked up more survivors. We had aircraft flying overhead helping us find the guys in the water.

The other three cruisers barely made it over to Tulagi. Two had lost their bows. The Japanese were really good with torpedoes. Those cruisers had independent double bulkheads, so when the Japanese hit the bows with their torpedoes, the crews were able to seal off those forward areas, and the ships didn't sink. So those cruisers had no bows on them, all lucky shots, their bows shot off, and they came into Tulagi. They were really sitting ducks and couldn't go very fast, and if the Japs had had good aircraft they could have gotten all of them. The amazing thing was that they fixed up these cruisers with temporary wooden bows. They made beams and planks from trees they'd cut down in the jungle, and in two days they had these wooden bows on those cruisers so they could make their way back to Noumea, or to somewhere where they had facilities to fix them up with regular steel bows. While they were working on these cruisers at Tulagi, we were afraid the Japanese would come in with air raids and try to sink them, but we didn't get any air raids, and the cruisers left with those wooden bows.

When we were on patrol, I had to know what was going on immediately ahead of me. I was on the radio listening and talking all the time, and I was always telling everyone else what I was doing. The radio was in the compartment right below where I stood when I was driving the boat. And there were headphones and a hand microphone to talk into that ran up to where I was standing, and so I'd be driving the boat and talking and listening on the radio. We were most effective because we were there, not because we did so much. But we showed. We were the Navy that showed. It's not that we sunk a lot of Jap ships, but just the fact that we were there, and that the Japanese had to be thinking of us as a possible threat. That made a difference. A lot of times they had to get the hell out of there because they didn't want to deal with us.

You know, we didn't talk a hell of a lot about when something happened to someone we knew. They were just gone, and we wrote them off and didn't do much about it. We just shut it off. I never looked at the empty cots or all that stuff you see in movies. If people got hurt, they flew out most of them. We'd take them over to Guadalcanal, and they'd fly them out. Tulagi was a lousy place to try and treat the wounded. If they didn't fly you out, you were dead.

You learned in the service how to protect yourself. And even when you're out with a boat in the middle of the ocean and there's guns going off all over, you learned that you do your job and you try to stay alive. You know, I never thought of that. And I found that the guys who thought about getting killed, they ended up getting killed. It was surprising. The ones that had that mental attitude, for whatever reason, they ended up getting killed.

One time when we were out on patrol, we were sent to check out a PT boat, the 43, Charlie Tilden's boat. It had been destroyed, and its remains had washed up on the beach. It was hit and ended up there, and I took a photo of it. They were hit by destroyer gunfire, which did a pretty good job on that thing. Charlie and most of his crew survived, and only a few were killed. We were sent to check it out and to see if we could get anything useful out of it. We didn't find anything we could use.

PT 43, with Charlie Tilden as skipper, was severely damaged in combat and run aground on Guadalcanal in early 1943. PT base force personnel scramble over the wreckage to see if anything could be salvaged.

PT boats were not designed for what we used them for. We lost an awful lot of people to small arms fire going up against Japanese barges in the Solomons. The Japanese would move all their people in small barges and things like that. And they'd have, maybe, thirty guys with small-caliber guns in each barge. We'd come up to them, and all hell would break loose from their individual guns. And we lost a lot of people trying to sink those barges, and we were not equipped for it. I mean, we had machine guns and 40mm cannons on the back of the boat, but PT boats stood up from the water, maybe six feet, and we had 3,000 gallons of high octane gas aboard. And we had depth charges and torpedoes, and it was bad because PT boats were such easy targets, standing up like that in the water. The Japanese barges were almost flat with the water, and you've got all that gunfire, and it was just a stupid thing to use PT boats for that purpose. And it was done during the whole war. It was worse in Hollandia, in New Guinea, and that area. And in the Philippines it was the same. There was no sense to it. I mean, why didn't they figure out some kind of a gunboat with armor on it and put it down in the water so that it wasn't such a big target. I mean, we were standing six feet above the water with no protection whatsoever. It was ridiculous. I saw a lot of those barges, and that really started there in the Solomons in 1942. We even tried to figure out how to put some armor on our boats out there, which was impossible. We were trying to make concrete or steel panels, but nothing really worked. So we had a lot of losses, but I was lucky.

The barge stuff really started with us, but we didn't get into it, thoroughly, until we got up the line a little and the Japanese were moving from one island to another, and they were moving in barges. They didn't do that in the beginning around Guadalcanal. We saw a couple, but they didn't use them regularly. They became a regular part of the deal in 1943. When we first got there in 1942 we were in the big ship operations at that point. And we weren't screwing around with barges. The only time in the war that PT boats were really effective—for the purpose that they were made—was at Guadalcanal. And from then on they were fighting barges, and they never fought major ships ever again. Or rather they fought them again in Leyte Gulf, but they had problems.

*Dave with PT boat squadron insignia with Japanese flags representing warships sunk by PT boats in the battle for Guadalcanal, December, 1942.*

But most of the time we were doing nothing. We slept during the day, so that we could be awake at night. And the Japanese only came down with their ships in the dark of the moon, because they were afraid of our aircraft, and in the dark of the moon they could come down and not get shot at by our airplanes. So we only had, maybe, ten days in a month when they would come down. So, the rest of the time, we were out on patrol, but we didn't expect anything. I used to turn on our main radio and listen to music from San Francisco. There were beautiful nights out there in the Pacific with the stars out and the moon out, and there were little tropical islands all around that you could see for miles. We knew the Japs wouldn't come out on those nights, so we could relax, or I'd go to sleep in the back of the boat.

Torpedo alcohol played a big part in what was happening. The torpedo alcohol was 180 proof, pure grain alcohol, and it burned when it went down. We got it in 55 gallon drums. It ran torpedoes; it was the fuel for the torpedoes. But when we didn't have to go out on patrol, those kids used to drink that goddamn stuff by the glasses full, usually with grapefruit juice. One night in early 1943 there was a truckload of 55 gallon drums on Tulagi being transferred from a supply ship to the boats, and that truckload got lost. And can you imagine how many people got drunk then?

Then they decided they were going to stop us from drinking it by putting gasoline into it. And the kids just determined that they could make stills and distill it. That's how we got the gasoline out. I had the most beautiful still in the world on my boat, but I didn't know it. It was under the floorboards. And my crew used all the best materials to build it. They had stills going all the time. I would make inspections and miss the still. I knew something was going on since they would share it with me, but I didn't bother them.

When the crew got a little rambunctious we took care of it, but, you know, when they had the alcohol from the torpedo tubes and everything else going, there was bound to be some trouble. I was on a first name basis with the crew, but I kept somewhat of a distance. I thought you had to. You'd figure that way I didn't know what they were doing, but I did know. And they just called me "Skipper" or "Mr. Hogan," and I got along great with everybody in the service.

I had some very interesting people on my crew. They were mostly a bunch of young kids. One was from Tennessee, and he was a real redneck kid who thought that pineapple grew with a hole in the middle of it. And he was a good kid but damned ornery. He was good at his job, but he didn't know from nothing. I had a machinist mate who was an older man, maybe thirty-six years old at the time, and his name was Homer Facto. He was a little short guy, but he absolutely knew how to handle machinery and to handle the young guys on the boat, and they looked up to him. He had

43

spent his life in the Adirondack Mountains, at Saranac Lake, taking care of speedboats. So he had a real feeling for the PT boats and what it took to put them together and keep them going. He was the most valuable guy I ever had. All the younger guys would do anything he told them. They looked up to him. He was so good. Sometimes we had to change engines, and he'd change the engines over in one night. And he'd have those kids working and have that boat ready the next morning. He was marvelous. As a result of it, we had the fastest boat in the squadron. He just had a feeling for it. A lot of the men didn't, but he did. He ended up back in the Adirondack Mountains, and he built a billiard parlor. He painted it like it was in the Navy—all grey enamel paint. The whole damn thing inside was grey enamel paint. I came to visit him, one time, and he was marching with a group of kids in some kind of a small drum and bugle corps. He wrote me for years after the war. Once he wrote me, and he said, "You know, I had two Skippers in the service. I had you and Kennedy. But you were the best." He was a great guy.

A few of the skippers were exceptional, Mark Wertz, Hugh Robinson, and Leonard "Nick" Nikoloric. Jack Searles had been a swimmer in college and I had been a lifeguard, and the first thing I'd had to do was race him in the pool. Of course he beat me, because he had been trained as a racer. So I knew him almost from the beginning. His brother, Bob Searles, was a year or so older, and he was a very quiet guy. He made no noise. We didn't even know that he was there. He had a lot of friends in the Navy. The Searles brothers had been in the Navy earlier, and they knew John Bulkeley [the PT boat skipper who evacuated MacArthur from the Philippines on his boat] and all those characters. Some of them had been in PTs in Hawaii at the beginning of the war, guys like Wertz and Charlie Tilden. And I got in on the next wave of people. So, they were the hotshots when I started. I ended up splitting time with Jack Searles and his crew on PT 59 when I first got there. The 59 was my boat, but they were short of boats, so two crews would share one boat and go out every other night, and Searles and I shared the 59. Then there were the Two Robinsons. We called one "Big Robbie," which was Hugh, because he was tall, about 6'2"; and the other was "Little Robbie." Big Robbie had graduated from the Naval Academy. After the war the Navy sent him to law school. Later, since Hugh knew French, they sent him to Paris, and he was a naval attache' in the embassy there. Then he was in Washington, and had a great deal there. When I was trying a big case in Washington, he came to all my parties, and I've followed him ever since.

*Crew of PT 59 en route to the South Pacific on board the USS Roger Williams, October, 1942. Back row right to left: Mitchel, Blalock, Tanchoco, Homer Facto, and Robert Nanney (later killed on PT 37 near Guadalcanal); front row: skipper Dave Levy, Wiltgens, Ostrander, and Kaiser. Ostrander is holding the Disney-designed squadron insignia: an angry mosquito guiding a torpedo, representing PT boats as "mosquito boats" for their small size, evasive maneuverability, and "bite".*

We had some other "trade school guys." You know, Annapolis was the trade school. So if you went through Annapolis, we said you went to the trade school. We indicated that they didn't learn anything there in trade school, but we got along with some of them. There were some real interesting ones, and some bummers. But they were good for big ships. They knew Navy regulations and how to live that way. That's what they taught them in there, at Annapolis.

*Skippers Hugh "Big Robbie" Robinson (left, commanding officer of squadron 3) and Bob Searles hold PT boat squadron insignia, Tulagi, early 1943.*

Then we had the Ivy League guys. It was amazing but the PT boat officers were loaded with people from Princeton and Harvard, and all those Ivy League schools. I had never had a lot of contact with those people before. So I got to know most of them one way or another. What happened was that so many of these Ivy League guys already knew each other. So they had a head start on us. You know, like in our squadron. Searles knew Nikoloric, and they knew maybe ten guys in PT boats. And they all had played sports together. So you had to sort of fight their club a little. Not that they made the rest of us miserable, but all their friends had the inside track, and I started on the outside until I finally got into their group. In the end it didn't make any difference. But some guys never made it into that group. The reason I made it is that I was an operator, and also I was in the Solomons almost before anybody else. And they all looked up to me because I had lived through that. But it was like a club for them, and this club did a lot to enhance each other's reputations, and I never went for that. Some of these guys got the Silver Star while they were in Washington, just because they knew the right people. Some of that "old school" stuff was sickening.

The Searles brothers, Jack and Bob, were from Princeton. They were in this group of about six guys from Princeton, and initially they weren't very friendly. But they recognized that I was an operator, and that's how I got along with them. I shared a room with one of them in Nassau, in the Caribbean, one time.

We had some good skippers there with us in the Solomons. Les Gamble had a good record. He was one hell of a good PT boat guy. He was highly respected. He married a very rich girl in Hawaii after the war and raised pineapples. "Stilly" Taylor came from a wealthy family. He had raced sailboats down the Atlantic coast to the Caribbean, so he had that sailing background that worked well for him in PT boats. He was good with girls. He had movie actresses come down and visit him in Panama. He was the only guy in Panama who had a car. He wasn't a bad guy but was kind of spoiled. He had a brother I got to know later, after the war, in Aspen, and we skied together.

Clark Faulkner was a hotshot, a good PT boat operator. He knew those guys from Princeton and was kind of in with them. Bart Connolly was an Annapolis grad, a good PT boat operator. Ralph Richards was a nice guy. And then there was Al Harris. He was a regular Navy reserve officer, the only one we had. He came from Watertown, and John Bulkeley was also from Watertown. I didn't particularly get along with John Clagett. He was one of those "trade school guys." When we were in the Russell Islands and I ran my boat onto the reef, he made it be known that I'd run it aground, but didn't mention I'd been able to save the boat and get it off the reef. He made me out to be a bad PT boat operator, and I didn't appreciate that. Another skipper was a guy named Bill Kreiner from Buffalo. His father was wealthy. He sold stuff they make beer out of. One time Kreiner had to pick up Admiral Halsey and take him somewhere, and he got there late and Halsey raised hell, and Kreiner got his father to get him out of PT boats.

Rollin "Westy" Westholm was the commander of Squadron 2 at one point. He wrote everything up like he was the commanding admiral. He had records of everything. He was the one who kept me back an extra three or four days because I didn't make the ship to return from New Zealand. He never went to New Zealand. And he wrote up every small, unimportant event. He kept such accurate records he knew where he was all the time. Jim Cross was a Southerner from Louisiana, and he also went to Princeton. He had problems with blacks, even though he used to tell stories about fooling around with black girls.

Frank Freeland was one of the skippers who got killed, along with most of his crew. Big Robbie was with him that night and said Frank's boat was hit by Japanese gunfire, and that he left too fast after he fired his torpedoes. The Japs saw his wake and got him. Another skipper was Charlie Tilden. He was a good guy and knew what was going on. Bob Wark was another of the Princeton group. They must have had a naval reserve unit there, and they all got in early and got into PT boats. Brent Greene was a lot of fun. We had a good time in Panama, but he wasn't a particularly good PT boat operator. There was a friend of Greene's we called "Louie Lopez." His name was actually Joe Kernell. In Panama Louie went into a whorehouse, knocked on a door and opened it up, and there was another guy in bed with one of the women. And Louie announced that the guy had violated the law by parking a car out in front of the place, and he said, "You're an officer. Do your duty and move your car." So the guy got up, and then Louie jumped into the sack with the woman. Louie and Greene were fun to be around. I spent a lot of time together with all those guys, from Newport in training, down to Panama, and then in the Solomons.

We had a couple of officers who I thought were real dumb. I kept away from them as much as I could. I mean, real dumb. But there were several of them that I have a lot of respect for. Big Robbie was squadron commander. He was a sharp guy, and I used to follow him in his boat. He knew what he was doing and he was bright. And then there was a guy I had the absolute, utmost respect for of anybody who was in the service, and he was one of my best friends. His name was Mark Wertz. He was an engineer. He had gone to Lehigh and was in engineering, and he had designed bridges. He was a big, tall, blonde guy, a football player, and he never swore. And the swearing out there was atrocious, but he never swore. He was married, and he had the opportunity to go with us to New Zealand on leave, and of course we tore the place apart. But he didn't go because he was married. He stayed there, at Tulagi, and didn't go because he realized what was going to happen when we got to New Zealand. I thought he was a real man. After the war he went back and worked on bridges and stuff like that. He never made a lot of money but he enjoyed life, and he just died this year, which is something. I did finally meet Wertz's wife. I knew her really well. He had his babies while I was in Newport, and I was the uncle of the babies. The wild uncle!

One of the skippers who got to Tulagi about a month after I did was Huck Wood. And just to give you an idea of the league I was in with these PT boat skippers, Huck's father had gone to Annapolis and was captain of a cruiser, the USS *Montpelier*. In February, 1943, Huck saw some American cruisers going by Tulagi, and one of them was the *Montpelier*, so he went up to it in his PT boat to say hello to his father. His father was a lot shorter than Huck, so when Huck got up on the ship and picked up his father to hug him, he knocked his father's cap off twice. He did this right in front of the admiral of the task force, who was also on the *Montpelier*. The admiral thought this was funny, and Huck's father introduced him.

Well, a couple of months later Huck was informed that his father had fallen down a hatch on his ship and had bled to death from an old appendix scar. And not more than a week after that, we got word on the radio that Huck was to stand by in his boat, PT 124, out in Tulagi harbor at 11:10 a.m. the next day. Huck didn't have any idea what was going on, but he got out there the next day, and, about 11 a.m., four of our destroyers came steaming into the harbor going about 25 knots. They were really moving. They slowed down a little bit as they did a wide turn around the harbor, and Huck was able to get his PT boat up next to the one in the lead, and he went aboard. The commanding officer greeted him as he boarded, and he asked Huck if he was Captain Leighton Wood's son. That was his dad's name, "Leighton", and Huck's too, but he'd been "Huck" since childhood. So Huck says, "Yes, Captain Leighton Wood was my father." And the officer introduced himself as Arleigh Burke, commander of the destroyer force in the Solomon Islands. He was on a mission but took time to stop by Tulagi to tell Huck that he had a lot of admiration for his father, and he said the Navy had lost a great officer, and he had lost a great friend. And that was that. "Thirty-one Knot Burke" had to get going on his mission. So Huck got back on the 124, and the destroyers took off. That shows you the connections some of these PT boat skippers had in the Navy.

Jack Searles was a personal friend of Admiral Halsey's son. They were together at Princeton. One time Searles gave Halsey a ride on his PT boat somewhere, and Halsey was asking Searles what he thought he should do about his son, who had a girlfriend back in Noumea. Halsey was worried that his son would marry her. I think Searles told him to just transfer the boy somewhere else. So here is one of our PT boat skippers counseling Admiral Halsey about a problem with his son.

Another guy on the boats was Lem Skidmore, and he later became a lawyer too. His father was a lawyer. He was an interesting guy. He was the dirtiest guy that ever lived in the PT boats. He never took a bath. It got so disgusting we had to throw him in the water to clean him up. His father was sort of a famous lawyer in New York, and Lem went to Princeton too. He was with that crowd. And, when we were in New Zealand, he went out with Maori girls, and he picked the lousiest looking girl you could find. We figured she was dirty enough to be with him. And he was a character, a bright, nice guy. He was tall, yeah, tall and thin. When we were kidding and talking, he'd come up with the craziest conversation.

Another group I thought was really exceptional were the coast watchers; they were really something. I got to know a couple of them, and you have to realize what kind of environment they were operating in. There would be one or two of them together out in some remote location, with three or four natives, and you never knew for sure if you could trust the natives, but the coast watchers couldn't have operated without their help. They'd get on the radio and give information on ship movements or airplanes, and the Japanese were waiting for that signal, so the coast watchers had to move away as soon as they put out that report. And, they did it every day! They were some guys. They were wonderful in that they were able to stay alive. They were mostly Australian, and some New Zealanders. The ones I knew were Australians, and we all knew them. They used to have good whiskey. We got very friendly with them. They were fun, real jolly guys. They were dirty though. They never took a bath.

We were supposed to have sunk many, many ships with our PT boats, but I think we might've sunk a couple. You know, we had torpedoes that were poor. And we didn't have the opportunities to really do it. I got some torpedo shots off, but I honestly don't know if I ever hit anything. You look for an explosion and all that. It's pretty damn dark, and you're worried about getting the hell out of there. We had radar, and our radar wasn't that good. But we had it first before the Japs, and that made the difference. We were able to see things on the radar, but you couldn't determine who was who. But the Japanese had good torpedoes.

I had loved to walk before the war, but you just couldn't walk anywhere in the Solomons. You could walk maybe a hundred yards into the jungle, and you were sweating and wet and your feet were wet and everything else, so you'd turn around. I never had the feeling before that I was so limited and that I couldn't get anyplace. I realized you just couldn't go through that jungle. And I really respected the Marines for going through that goddamned jungle. But there were guys there who had hobbies. There was one guy whose hobby was birds. He had a small gun, and he used to go out shooting those birds, and he sent them all back to some museum somewhere. He had all kinds, every kind of bird that was there. And he had a ball shooting birds.

We used to see the Marines around Tulagi all the time. And every once in awhile, we had to go to Guadalcanal, over to Henderson Field. We'd take somebody over there or back, or go pick something up.

I had Admiral Halsey on my boat twice. Once Halsey came off a ship, and I picked him up and took him over to Guadalcanal. And I talked to him a little, and he was interesting. He was a good help to us, you know. We ended up getting the Presidential Unit Citation, and he got us in on that. He was interested in PT boats, and he wanted to find out what we were doing. He had a reputation for being kind of a fiery guy and for using a lot of salty language, but he was a softy in a lot of ways. But he was a rah-rah guy, and he wasn't like some of the other top brass. Some of those guys were sort of goofy, I think.

You know, when we were out on patrol, we knew when something was going to happen, so we weren't at the ready every minute, because there was no reason to be at the ready since we knew our territory, and we knew what was going on. I had a couple of admirals out with me once, and there were planes flying around off in the distance. Immediately they started yelling, "Man your guns." And I knew there was no reason to do it because I'd been there for a while and could recognize which planes were ours and which were theirs. The planes that day were ours, so I knew we were safe. But they outranked me and were convinced that the planes were Japanese, so they started giving stupid orders. There was so much stupidity amongst some of those older officers. They didn't really have a feel for what was going on.

The crew cooked and ate on the boat, but I either ate on the tender *Jamestown* or ashore. We had a mess cook, but he was trained to be on a big ship. He was a nice guy—he was all right—but I don't think he liked the action. We had a lot of Spam, and, well, there wasn't much to cook. We had the PT boat tender there, the big old yacht *Jamestown*, and the crews were sometimes eating on the *Jamestown*. The *Jamestown* was a huge yacht of somebody's that they converted into a tender. You know, it was a couple of hundred feet long. It was a big ship. They had it all camouflaged with a lot of tree limbs and things all over it to make it hard to pick out from the air. You know Tulagi was in the goddamn jungle, and we slept with mosquito nets. And so you did everything to protect yourself from the jungle. If I wasn't sleeping on the *Jamestown*, I'd sleep ashore in a hut. There were several buildings there, like native huts. They weren't great. They were all made of local materials, thatching. There were maybe ten officers staying in this one hut. Jack Kennedy and Lenny Thom were staying there.

Nobody in the PT boats really paid any attention to Navy regulations, so in the Solomons everyone wore whatever they damn well pleased. Some of the guys, like Kennedy, would run around all the time without a shirt on, and he liked hats and he had a whole collection of hats and he'd usually be wearing one. I'd gotten hold of an Air Corps flight suit, you know, a one-piece jump suit, and I'd wear that most of the time. I kept covered up enough so that I didn't ever really get sunburned.

Then there was the last night that the Japanese left Guadalcanal (February 7/8, 1943). They'd started evacuating their troops a few nights earlier and a few of our boats got sunk. So they told us to just monitor what they were doing. They came in with destroyers to pick up as many of their guys as they could. And we knew they were going to leave then because we had their code. The Navy thought that they were going to take the troops around to another part of Guadalcanal—on the back side. So they put us out along the back side and let them get on their ships. And we had lost so many PT boats by then, the Navy didn't want us to directly attack the enemy ships.

Big Robbie was ahead of me and I was behind him. There were only two of us, and we were on the other side of the island from where all the activity was. A Japanese float plane came over and started to bomb us. A bomb landed, oh, maybe a hundred feet from my boat. And it could have done a pretty good bit of damage if it had come even a little closer, even without hitting me. We never got hit, and the plane had enough bombs to go after Robbie too. We were trying to get into places impossible for the plane to get us, close to the shore.

The next morning, as it got light, we headed back around toward Tulagi. We went past where the Japs had been loading their guys on destroyers, off the northwest coast of Guadalcanal. Their destroyers were all gone. They'd had to leave in a hurry as it got light, because they were worried about getting attacked and sunk by our airplanes. And as we got there, we saw all kinds of Japanese in the water. They weren't able to get them all aboard the destroyers, and they just left them floating there in the water. I picked up seventeen of them and put them up on the bow of my boat, had them sitting there, and we took them back to Tulagi. I thought it was sensible, because we could capture them and be successful in doing something, finally. I was the only guy who did it, and I was probably stupid to do it. So we got them back to the base, and the Marines were mad as hell when I got in there. And they took control. They took those Japs off our boat, and I don't know what happened to them. I think they may have taken them out and shot them. But it was amazing to be out there in our boat, just floating around among all those Japs in the water and picking them up. There were Japanese all over in the water. There must've been 500 of them out there floating around. I guess some had swum out from shore, and there were some in small boats. The Japanese navy just left them, because they had to get out of the way of our planes coming up the next morning. We didn't shoot any of those Japs in the water. They'd had it, and they weren't going to fight.

*Japanese POWs on the bow of PT 59, picked up on the morning of February 8, 1943, after they had been left in the water on the final night of the Japanese evacuation of Guadalcanal.*

When the Japanese pulled out and left all those guys in the water, we found a Japanese officer's boat left out there, and we brought it back to cruise around in. There were also flags in the water, and I picked one up. It was with some other stuff. They had packs that they just threw in the water. So a few of us had our photo taken with the flag, and then I sent that flag to my cousin. He's now a doctor in Washington, and he still has that flag.

*PT boat skippers and officers pose with Japanese flag Dave picked up from the waters of Iron Bottom Sound between Guadalcanal and Tulagi by PT 59 on February 8, 1943, the morning of the final Japanese evacuation from Guadalcanal. Photo was taken on February 11, 1943 in front of the briefing hut at Sesapi, Tulagi. Note PT boat squadron insignia over the door in background. Back row, left to right: Nick Nikoloric, Dave Levy, unknown, Lem Skidmore, Stilly Taylor, unknown; front row: Joe "Louie Lopez" Kernell, Solomon islands native holding flag, unknown, unknown.*

*Dave Levy poses with Japanese flag he plucked out of the water on February 8, 1943.*

*Dave sent the flag to his cousin, Teddy Amdursky, back in Rochester and it made the local paper on April 22, 1943.*

On the last night of the Japanese evacuation of Guadalcanal, an abandoned Japanese launch was recovered by one of the PT boats. PT skippers Mark Wertz and Dave Levy are shown here cruising around in the launch in Tulagi harbor in late February, 1943.

# 5: NEW ZEALAND

*After the Japanese evacuation of Guadalcanal in early February, 1943, things quieted down around Tulagi. With no more Japanese troops to supply on Guadalcanal, the Tokyo Express stopped running, and there wasn't much for the PT boats to do. But they had been in nearly constant combat for several months, and the nerves of the skippers and crews were frayed. Some "Rest & Recreation" was in order, so arrangements were made for trips to New Zealand. Other Marine units had also been taking leaves there. The PT boat personnel were divided up into groups for their leaves. They were heading to European-style islands with all the amenities of the U.S., incredible scenery, and reputedly the most friendly women in the entire Pacific.*

So around late February of 1943 I had leave in New Zealand. I was in the second group that went down there on leave. The first group went with the Marines, and when they got back we talked to them about all the things they did, and they told us what girls to go with. I got into a New Zealand hotel and was with one of these girls within a half hour of the time I got there. So that was the good news, but the bad news was that, with all the exertion, I injured myself, and it put me out of commission. But it was very cordial down there. The New Zealand women were very accommodating. You would walk down residential streets in Auckland and there were Marine uniforms hanging on wash lines all over the place, so that tells you what was going on. All the New Zealand men were away fighting in the desert.

*Dave on leave, South Island, New Zealand near Mt. Cook, early March, 1943.*

While I was there I decided to climb the highest mountain in New Zealand, Mount Cook, down on the South Island. I also wanted to fish, but it was the wrong season. So I checked into the hotel they have there by the mountain, the Hermitage they called it, and I was the only man in the hotel with forty-five women—teachers. So I struggled with my condition!

I carried skis up there on Mount Cook. I didn't get to the top, but I got up to where there was a stone hut, and I went with a guy who was a pretty good climber. But I had been at sea level in the tropics and couldn't handle the altitude. I got up there at 4 o'clock in the afternoon, and I was so tired I just went to bed and walked down the next day.

I had a great time down there at Mount Cook, but I got back to Auckland a day late, and I didn't realize I was late. I was told to be back on a certain day, and I got back on that day, but the ship had left, and I missed it. So I reported to the admiral and the admiral confined me to the hotel. He yelled at me, "You're going to stay at that hotel. Now, you stand by there so I know where I can get hold of you and get you on a ship and back to your unit. You stay there." So next thing I know I'm at that hotel, and I went into the bar and ended up meeting a lady in there whose husband was a high-ranking officer in the New Zealand Army. He was fighting the war in the desert.

I finally caught up with the ship in New Caledonia and got back to Tulagi. And the commander of our squadron, "Westy" Westholm, was so upset I missed the ship that he kept me in Tulagi a few weeks longer than I was supposed to be at the end of my tour.

# 6: THE RUSSELL ISLANDS

*Though the Japanese had been driven from Guadalcanal, they still occupied the central and northern islands of the Solomons chain. Foiled in their efforts to build an airfield on Guadalcanal, they began building another one farther north, on the island of Munda in the central Solomons. The Marines and U.S. Army geared up for another island invasion, this time to secure the Japanese airfield at Munda. To support the landing, the Tulagi PT boats were shifted north to a temporary base at the old Lever Brothers plantation on one of the Russell Islands. The Tokyo Express wasn't effectively running during this time, so the PT boats had mostly uneventful patrols in and around the Russells and nearby Munda. It was almost relaxing, as the PT boat skippers moved into a comfortable plantation house and whiled away the daylight hours between nighttime patrols by playing endless hours of poker.*

After I got back to the Solomons from New Zealand, they sent us up to the Russell Islands, a ways north and west of Guadalcanal. They put us up at a plantation, and there were well-maintained buildings, a big house, and a nice lawn around everything. It had been kept up real well. When we first went in to the Russell Islands, I went ashore and everything was very peaceful. There wasn't anything to do, so I decided to take a nap. I was lying there on the grass in the plantation front yard, napping, and I look up and there's two native soldiers in shorts. They looked at me, and I was a little startled. They were watching me. They didn't know who the hell I was. They were surprised because the Japs had just left, and we had just gotten there. I guess they didn't expect to see any Americans, and there I was taking a nap.

At the Russells, the crew was on the boats, and the officers were all in the big house. It was like a club. We didn't have a lot of whiskey, but we did have some alcohol. There was even a dock where we could re-fuel the boats.

*After their crews returned from leave in New Zealand, a group of PT boats from Tulagi was moved forward to the Russell Islands in March, 1943. The skippers occupied an abandoned Lever Brothers plantation house. Night patrols were mostly uneventful, and there was a lot of time for what Dave termed "continuous bull sessions" as depicted in this photo. Upper left is Lem Skidmore holding a deck of cards, Dave Levy is at lower left, and Jim Cross is at lower right.*

We had one event in the Russell Islands that was sort of funny. We had a Marine contingent of antiaircraft gunners, and they were stationed there with us to protect our boats. Well, we were playing poker constantly, except when we'd have to go out at night on the boats, but we wouldn't go out every night, so it was comfortable. We really got into one of these Marines, and he owed us thousands of dollars. Well, he got orders to ship out, and we didn't want him to move until we could collect from him. So we took the breech mechanism out of his gun, and we knew that he wouldn't leave without that. He finally made some deal with us so he could pack up his gun and leave. It was fun there.

The worst thing that happened to the 59 boat happened while we were at the Russell Islands. We were out on patrol, it was after midnight, and my crew wanted to get some freshwater into our tanks on the boat. We'd get freshwater from our destroyers, and the crew said they thought they saw a destroyer close by, even though it was complete darkness. So they kept saying, "Let's pull over there and get some freshwater." So I started to go over to where they thought they'd seen the destroyer, and it turned out to be a little island, and I ran the boat up on the coral reef surrounding that little island.

We went up on that reef so hard that you could get out of the boat and walk on the coral. We didn't ruin too much on the boat, but we had a hole where the coral punched through the hull. This was not good, because if we couldn't save the boat we'd have to abandon it and burn it when we left, and the squadron would have one less PT boat. We'd already had so many losses we really didn't want to lose another boat. So I took an anchor rope about 400 or 500 feet long, with an anchor on the end of it, and put it over my shoulder and walked out to the end of the reef in my boots. I figured I'd hook the anchor to the edge of the reef, and then the crew would pull on the rope and drag the boat off the reef. Well, when I stepped off the edge of the reef, the damn anchor caught me and took me down, and I had to get out from under it. While I was underwater, I got it hooked on the reef, but I got caught under the rope and couldn't get free. It was holding me under water, plus I had my boots on, so it was hard to swim. I had a hell of a time getting out, and

I thought I was going to drown. I finally got free of the rope and came to the surface and climbed back up on the reef. Then the guys on the boat pulled on the rope, and we slid the boat off the reef into the deep water. Everybody on the boat was pulling on that rope. I think that was about the closest I got to getting killed in the war, and it would have been by drowning.

So then we were back in the water and it was getting light, and we had a bailer running because water was coming in through the hole in the hull. As long as we went at a decent speed, the bailer was able to stay ahead of the water. But if we had stopped we would have sunk. We radioed Tulagi, which was maybe 50-60 miles away. We got there later that morning, and they had a couple of metal rigs that they were able to sink underneath the boat, and then float them and put the boat up on it like a dry dock. They got the boat fixed in about two hours, and we drove back to the Russell Islands, all before it got dark. We all thought, "Geez, that could have been a lot worse." Of course the other skippers were giving me grief about that mishap, but it was my luckiest day on the boat.

About this time there was an Army Reserve group from New England they brought into Munda one night, and the Japanese got up in those tall trees and yelled and screamed all night long. And finally that Army Reserve group was pulled out. They weren't able to take it. The Reserve officers were no good. I think the only reason they got into the Reserves was to get paid. The Army never let it be known, and they sent all the officers down to another island and tried to re-train them, but I don't think they ever got them re-trained. I talked to someone who was in that unit who told me about this.

There were a lot of things in the Russells that were sort of unusual. We were relaxed because there were no Japanese, and we just lived in the plantation house; and we were living pretty good. It's amazing that we were able to keep our senses enough to be able to do things properly with the PT boats, because we were absolutely goofy there in the Russells.

*An evocative urinal behind the plantation house at the Russell Islands.*

# 7: KENNEDY

*Before the PT squadrons moved to the Russells, a new group of replacement PT boat skippers and crews showed up at Tulagi in April of 1943. One of them was Jack Kennedy. To Dave, he was just another Ivy League PT boat skipper. He'd learned to deal with the others he'd met from Princeton and elsewhere, so he didn't think Kennedy was too much different from the rest of them. But Kennedy proved to be engaging and pleasant and made friends easily. Though Dave still fought the discrimination he encountered for being Jewish, Kennedy mostly kidded him about it, and they became friends. As Dave was rotated back to the States at the end of his combat tour later in 1943, he turned over his boat, PT 59, to Kennedy, who had lost his boat, the 109. It had been rammed and sunk by one of the Japanese destroyers of the Tokyo Express. Kennedy was instrumental in saving several of his crew, and led the effort to swim to a nearby island. Several harrowing days later, he and most of his crew were finally rescued. None of the PT boat skippers in the Solomons in 1943, least of all Dave, had any inkling that, in just seventeen short years, this incident would help propel Kennedy to the Presidency.*

Jack Kennedy showed up with some replacement crews in 1943. I met Kennedy and often talked with him over the month's time we were there together at Tulagi. Sometimes we called Kennedy "Shafty," because he would like to say, ". . . shafted again." But I usually just called him Jack. Another friend of Kennedy's was Lenny Thom. He was a college football player from the Big 10, Ohio State I think. He was a lot of fun, a nice guy, Lenny Thom. He was with Kennedy a lot. He was a big, tall, light-blondish sort of guy. He always had a joke. After they moved us up from Tulagi to the Russells, we were there for a while, and then I went back to Tulagi, and Kennedy and some of the others moved up to a new base at Rendova. They were operating out of there when he lost his boat, the 109.

They brought Kennedy and his crew back to Tulagi after they rescued them off the island they were stranded on, and I saw him there again. He never wanted to talk about it. He always felt that he had screwed up. But he did a wonderful job of saving the people off his boat. And, you know, he was a good swimmer, even with a horrendous back condition, and he really saved two guys. It happened on a dark, dark night. You couldn't see very much when you were out on your boat at night. I don't think he was at the wheel. I don't know, they never really discussed that. I don't think they saw the destroyer before it cut them in two, and this kind of collision was very unusual. It was the only one I know of. A lot of boats went aground because the charts were so lousy and you never knew where you were, but a PT boat colliding with a Jap destroyer, that was a unique event. I talked about it with a guy who was in another boat very close to Kennedy, Little Robbie. He said it was so black and dark you couldn't see a damn thing, and he said that he never blamed anybody for it. It could happen to anybody.

There was discussion among the PT boat skippers after this Kennedy thing that maybe they should have gone back to look for him. Apparently they thought he was dead and didn't go back, but later they thought they should have. It's only scuttlebutt, because I wasn't there at Rendova. But I knew what was going on at Tulagi. And they thought Kennedy and his crew were all dead. They didn't find out he was alive until that native brought something from the coast watcher. And that was two days after. They were on a small island. The reason they thought they should've gone back to look for him, even that night, was because they were out there floating around on the bow. The stern had sunk after they got rammed by the Jap destroyer. The only reason they started swimming was when it started getting light. They figured they'd better get off the bow, and that's when they started swimming to those islands.

I finally got Kennedy to talk about it later, and he was not proud of the whole thing. As a matter of fact, we kind of kidded him about it, and I joked that he was a "great Naval hero." So then he started to kid me back, and we were both calling each other "great Naval heroes." He wrote me several notes after that, and he used to kid me. He'd write, "To a great Naval hero." And I always pushed and kidded him about the hero business, because none of us gave a damn about being a hero. All the rest of us only wanted to get home. He was the only one who wanted to go back into combat after he'd lost his boat. And, you know, they would normally send them home, but he insisted on staying there and getting another boat.

I was going back to the States about that time, this was fall of 1943, so they assigned Kennedy my boat, PT 59. And in that boat after I left, he had his other adventure, where he got into a tight place and evacuated some trapped Marines. He did that in my old boat, with my crew. He thought that would make a name for himself for his wartime achievements, but it was the ramming and sinking of PT 109 that did it for him, and that always irked him a little, I think. So for years after that, when we'd correspond, we'd always refer to each other as "great Naval heroes." In fact, Kennedy came to Rochester one time after the war, and he made a speech. He recognized my wife, and he wrote a note to her, and the note said, "To the wife of a great Naval hero and my friend." And that's how we used to kid each other.

During that time my father got in touch with his father just to say ". . . my kid's out there with yours." And in the long run his father was no help to him, I'll tell you. Kennedy was an interesting character. He was well educated. He had spent time in Europe, in London, at the School of Economics, when his father was the Ambassador to England, and he really had a pretty good idea of world affairs. None of the rest of us knew anything. And he would say to me, I'll always remember, "You people," he said, "are all, ah, soft on Communism, aren't you?" And I was Jewish, and by that he meant Jewish people were soft on Communism. He was kidding me, of course, and we laughed about it. I was with him when his older brother Joe got killed in Europe. You couldn't really see the effect it had on Jack because he was so quiet. And he had another brother-in-law that got killed, and he was the only one left in the family in combat. His friends told me that his brother Joe was a great guy. His father wanted to make Joe president of the U.S. He gave that to Jack when Joe's plane went down.

# 8: NEWPORT

As the combat tours of the veteran PT boat skippers in the Solomons ended, they were rotated back to the U.S. Many were assigned to train new skippers and crews back where they got their start, at Newport, Rhode Island. After having lived through the nighttime battles around Guadalcanal, this new duty seemed like an extended rest and recuperation leave. The married skippers, like Hugh "Big Robbie" Robinson, brought their wives to live with them in Newport, while a group of the single officers, including Dave, rented one of the large Newport mansions on Third Beach. Some of the married officers called this house "The Snake Ranch," and it became known for the riotous parties that went on almost continuously. Jack Kennedy had stayed on in the Solomons after taking over Dave's boat, the 59. One night he pulled off a daring rescue under fire of a group of trapped Marines pinned down on an island shoreline. He thought this would make up for the episode where he lost PT 109. But his father realized the heroic efforts of his son to save his crew after the 109 was rammed and sunk were much more compelling than the Marine evacuation. So that was the story used to promote his wartime service in future political campaigns. By this time Kennedy's back injury had gotten worse. He was shipped home and hospitalized in the States, though he was soon well enough to come visit his fellow PT boat skippers in Newport from time to time, and get in on at least some of the parties.

I got sent back to the States in time for Christmas, 1943. When I left the Pacific, one good souvenir I took was the commissioning plaque off the 59. It was aluminum and said "Commissioned on . . ." and so forth. I brought that home with me, and I still have it. Later I had a duplicate made, which I sent to Jack Kennedy when he was president. I think it might be in his library in Boston.

I flew from Guadalcanal to Hawaii in a PBY, and had to stop at a number of islands en route—it's a long ways from the Solomons to Hawaii. I had something called "first possible transportation" orders, and when I got on this PBY I was the only passenger. I found out it was a special trip for me because of my orders. "Westy" Westholm, our squadron commander, set this up because he wanted me to buy Christmas gifts and send them home for the skippers still on Tulagi. The plane stopped in New Caledonia, Samoa, Christmas Island, and then went on to Hawaii. It was long trip, particularly in a PBY that wasn't very fast. It took a couple of days flying night and day. And then I flew from Hawaii to the States on the big Pan Am China Clipper flying boat. Those were great orders! I was able to sit down and eat at a table in that thing. I couldn't believe it, after being out in the Solomons in pretty primitive conditions eating Spam, there I am sitting on the China Clipper eating a fine dinner. That was first class treatment!

So I got to San Francisco and bought the gifts and sent them out to the families of the other skippers. Then I started going wild, as they say. I'd been out in the Pacific and in combat and in primitive conditions for a year, and I was determined to have fun in San Francisco. And in San Francisco, they didn't let the Navy enlisted people drink until 5:00 p.m., but they didn't stop the officers. I used to get started at one end and walk down the hall in the hotel and make dates. And I succeeded in having a good time.

So after that little break in San Francisco, I flew back to Rochester for Christmas, 1943.

*Dave received "first possible transportation" orders to get him home from the South Pacific to the States in November, 1943. This allowed him to fly the luxurious Pan Am China Clipper flying boat from Honolulu to San Francisco. This is his ticket and boarding pass for the flight on November 11, 1943.*

My father was very proud of me, but I didn't like how he was handling my connection to the Navy. When I flew in to Rochester from San Francisco via Detroit, he had five newspaper reporters there at the airport to talk to me. And I didn't talk to them. I refused. I said to them, I'm not a hero, those guys who are still out there are the heroes, and I'm not. I was mad at my dad for doing it. I think I was a little screwed up too. My dad realized then that I didn't want any special attention. So they put in the paper, "Modest hero returns." I didn't discuss PT boats with anybody for a hell of a long time. We weren't trying to be heroes, and we didn't think of ourselves that way. But the Searles brothers and the guys from Ron 3 came back to the states earlier that year, and the media made a lot of a few of them. The PT boat veterans accepted that they were being made heroes, and they made the best of it, going to parties and everything. Stilly Taylor, Bob Searles, and "Nick" Nikoloric were featured on the cover of *Life* magazine, May 10, 1943. We never discussed any of that stuff, even when I was teaching new crews at Newport.

After the Christmas break in Rochester, I got assigned to Newport as an instructor on PT boats. After Kennedy lost his boat, he took over the 59 from me, and then he got sent home a little later. He wasn't in real great shape physically, so they sent him to the Newport Naval Hospital, and he came and visited us a few times. The thing that surprised me is that he had the junkiest cars, the worst goddamned cars you could have. They came from his family's place over at Hyannis Port. They had some old cars there, and he drove them all.

There were a number of us combat veterans back from the Pacific there at Newport training the new guys. We rented a nine-bedroom house on the beach at Newport, but we had nothing to raise hell with, no booze. So we asked Kennedy to get us some scotch. His old man was importing scotch, and he sent a truckload of Haig and Haig Pinch to that house. They stacked up the cases in the kitchen so that you couldn't see out of the windows. After that, what happened in that place you couldn't believe. It was party all the time, and Kennedy would come over to visit us in that house. And the girls used to come from all around. They'd come in carloads, because we were the party house. And some of the wildest partyers in this house were our married guys. They were horrendous! But we would do training during the day, and party every night—it was one continuous party.

During this time we had a guy who was supposed to have impregnated a girl in Florida. We called him "Louie Lopez" because in Panama he talked like a Spaniard. Kennedy went down to Florida at one point, and he stopped and saw the PT boat guys stationed there, and they got a date for him. They wanted him to check on something. They asked him if he could figure out if one of the guys had impregnated this girl. This woman claimed that Louie had impregnated her, so they sent Kennedy on this date to look at the kid and talk to the woman. And Kennedy said, "This kid's the spittin' image of Louie." And that's all we needed to know, Louie was the father!

I was back in Newport for a long time, a year and a half, and we were training new crews. We never had the time to do any good training. We used to take them out into the Atlantic from Newport and let them ride around.

At one point I had a girlfriend there, a beautiful Spanish model from New York, and I soon discovered that she had the "crabs." She was so beautiful that I didn't let that stop me, but I had to keep getting treated. I'd show up every Monday morning at sick bay, and they'd spray me. I was well known there at sick bay. One time the doctor said to me, "You know how to get rid of the crabs, don't you? You douse the area with whiskey, and sprinkle it with sand. Then the crabs get drunk and stone each other to death."

# 9: THE PHILIPPINES

*Having returned to Newport after his service in the Solomons, Dave never thought he would have to face combat again. The Solomons PT boat skippers had become minor celebrities after their victories against the Japanese. Three of them, Bob Searles, Stilly Taylor, and "Nick" Nikoloric, were featured in a cover story in Life magazine. Later on Jack Kennedy would use his PT boat exploits in the Solomons to good advantage in campaigning for political office. They could all deservedly rest on their laurels, and many were given Stateside duty in their subsequent assignments. But in the Battle of Surigao Strait in the Philippines in 1944, the performance of the PT boats was viewed by the Navy as less than stellar. The solution they came up with was to send combat veteran PT boat skippers, many of whom had served so effectively at the beginning of the war in the Solomons, to the Philippines to further train the PT boat skippers and crews there. Dave was one of those skippers. He bade his comrades and the parties of Newport goodbye, and was soon on a cross-country train to California to catch a ship that would take him back across the Pacific.*

After a year and a half in Newport, they decided to send me back out to the Pacific. The PT boats really had a chance of doing some good when they were in the Philippines. The whole Navy was down there fighting the Japanese navy, but the commanders screwed up and put the PT boats in a position where they were facing the whole Japanese navy. Then the PT boats had some trouble at the Battle of Surigao Strait, and they blamed it on the fact that the officers and crews weren't well trained. So the idea was that they were going to take a bunch of us who had PT boat experience in the Solomons, and send us over there to train the crews in the Philippines. But by the time we got ready to go out there, the war was practically over. But I had my orders, and on the way I had to take a whole group of people across the country—PT boat people—who had been trained at Melville or who were being transferred from the Atlantic theater to the Pacific. I took them across the country to deliver them so that they could go to various places from San Francisco. I lost about twenty-five of them! We were on a big train, and I couldn't hold their hands. Some of them seemed to vanish along the way, but when I got the rest of them there, I turned them over to somebody and went out partying in San Francisco. I raised a lot of hell while I was waiting for the *Matsonia* to depart; it was a large cruise ship, and I got friendly with all the guys, and they told me what girls to look for. But I got tired of partying in San Francisco. I was partied out by the time I got ready to climb onboard that ship. I really didn't look around on the way to Hawaii, I slept most of the way. I woke up when we got to Hawaii, and the rest of the way I was alert. For the leg of the trip from Honolulu to the Philippines, we went by way of Hollandia in New Guinea. I threw away all my clothes before I got back on the ship in Honolulu, because I knew I could get clothes when I got there, and I went aboard with two seabags full of whiskey.

We used to go up on deck with a bottle of whiskey in the afternoon and sit in those deck chairs, and we acted like we owned the whole damned place. The ship was filled with Navy and Army people, and there must've been five or six thousand on that ship, and they pushed them all together. But there was a group of us Naval officers, and we were living in three-room suites, just three guys to a suite. Most of the rest of the people on the ship were stashed in bunks, but we lived high on the hog. The only thing wrong with that damn ship was that they turned off the freshwater for the showers, and we had to take showers in salt water, and I didn't like that. But what made up for it was that I spent most of the time with the Navy nurses. There were about fifty of them on the ship. The sailors used to get the nurses in the elevators on the ship and then turn the elevators off. But we could bring them back to our suites. I had been out in the Pacific before and knew where I was going, so I had a pretty good party. But we never talked war stories to them. You talked about where they were educated and where they lived, if they had boyfriends, and all that kind of stuff. The word got around that I'd been out in the Pacific before, and I answered like I'd been in it before. So that didn't hurt my chances—it was fun.

I was really in business with that whiskey. I traded for everything. I got to Hollandia and traded for a Jeep. I got a guy to take me out to a barge that was full of beer. And I got three hundred cases of Ranier beer for my whiskey. And I kept on using that as trading material. I was really operating.

On the *Matsonia*, on the way to Hollandia, a Navy nurse who was onboard the ship found out she was pregnant. She wanted to get an abortion out there in the Pacific, and she heard maybe I could arrange it with my whiskey to trade. Well, I asked around and I had the liquor to trade for it, but I decided it wasn't a good idea. It ended up that two dentists were offering to do it. I called it off, and she didn't get the abortion. They sent her home when we got to Hollandia.

Then from Hollandia we ended up in the Philippines, and I was there until the end of the war, near Leyte. I was in Squadron 23 when I went back out there. We didn't have much combat, we just did a lot of exercises, but I did a couple of combat missions. It wasn't much. I was made the executive officer, second in command. We had Higgins PT boats, and I hated them. They were not anywhere near as good as the Elco boats that we had in the Solomons. Those Elco boats were good boats.

We were set to go north for the invasion of Japan. But while I was there I did the craziest thing I ever did in the war. When the war was over in Europe, I went to one of those big USO shows and got drunk as a skunk. And I mean, really drunk! I walked away from the show, and there was a general's Jeep sitting there. And I got in the damn Jeep. And just by getting in the jeep I had a good chance of getting shot. But I not only got in, I started it up and took that jeep and went like hell. I realized right away I could get shot if they put out the word. So I immediately woke up to my situation when I started driving it. I probably should have gotten out of it right then and there, but I kept on going and took it down to the harbor and pushed it over into the water. Now, that was the goddamndest, dumbest thing that a man could do! This was after going through a whole war, and I was in more potential trouble than I think I was at any time during the war. I just thought it would be funny, I guess. It's hard to imagine now exactly what my thinking was there. But nobody saw me, and I got away with it. It sunk in later, and I didn't think it was funny. Of course now it's funny.

At the end of the war I was in Leyte. I was taken out of where I was, and they moved me down to Leyte Gulf. There was a big PT boat base there. I didn't like it, because it was going to keep me there. I was entitled to go home right away, but I stayed for awhile, and I set up the procedure for destroying the surplus boats and how to get any worthwhile equipment out of them. What we did was that we had the crews loosen all the nuts and bolts, so that, when we got the boat under a big crane, we could pick the engines and stuff up with the crane. Everything was supposed to be loose enough so that we could do it in a hurry, in a kind of assembly-line technique. And using this technique, we could do, maybe, ten boats in a day, or fifteen boats in a day. Then once we'd gotten the engines and other heavy stuff out of them, we pushed them up on the beach and burned them. The ones that were newer, we put them out on buoys and left them in the bay. We had maybe a hundred or so of them on buoys. But the rest of them we burned. I think I burned about 150 boats, and I didn't think anything about it. You'd have thought I'd have had some kind of emotional attachment to those PT boats, but I didn't care. I just wanted to go home.

The reason we burned them was that you had to be careful. There were Chinese in business in the Philippines when we were there. And they would buy anything, including whole sawmills. The whole goddamned thing would come in crates, shipped over for our use, and somebody would sell it to them, and it would end up on the mainland of China. And that's the kind of business that was going on. And that's the reason that we really burned the boats. We didn't want the boats to get into the hands of somebody like that, because they would've used the boats in their illegal businesses.

I did one other thing there in the Philippines, and it was this other thing that made me go into law after the war. By that time the war was over, and I was ready to come home, but I volunteered to do some legal work to see what it was like. I was chosen by the admiral to investigate a crime, and the crime was a stabbing in a whore house in the Philippines. An Army guy got stabbed, cut up pretty bad, and this happened in the middle of a big brawl near Leyte, and he didn't know who did it. So I was supposed to find out who did it. You know, who did what to whom? Well, I took a Navy yeoman and I went to the place and questioned everybody, maybe ten people. I took their testimony, and I was supposed to report to the admiral. It just kept running through my mind: who did what to whom? And I got more confused the deeper I got into it. There happened to be a black Navy mess guy involved, and the admiral was sure that the black guy did it, but I couldn't prove it. At the end I put in the report that I just couldn't find out, and I didn't tap the black guy. The admiral was a Southern gentleman, and he was sure that the black guy did it. So he wrote a bad fitness report for me as a result of it. It was the first bad one I had had in the service. And I challenged it. I said what I did and how I did it, and I had all the testimony and wasn't able to determine who did what to whom, and I answered the questions about that fitness report, and they expunged that whole thing from my record. So that was my start at being a lawyer.

At the end of the war I went all the way back to the States on a destroyer. The captain of this destroyer liked rare meat, and that's the first time I ever had rare meat. I was trying to get in with the captain by also eating rare meat. It took a while to get home. We went through Hawaii, but I didn't even get off the ship.

# 10: AFTER THE WAR

*Like many veterans returning home after World War II, Dave Levy had been changed by his experiences in the service. He had learned how to manage and to get along with diverse groups of people. He had acquitted himself well in combat, and had gained confidence in his abilities. And now he was motivated to succeed more than ever before. He decided on law school, something many of the PT skippers ended up doing. In addition to law, he pursued two lifelong passions, fishing and skiing, and made frequent trips from Rochester to his vacation house in Aspen, Colorado. For years he never talked about his PT boat experiences with anyone, even with his law school roommate who had served in PT boats in New Guinea. He attended PT boat reunions, but wartime experiences were rarely discussed. The veterans fell into their old ways of partying and drinking, and there wasn't a whole lot of interest in trading war stories. It was only much later that Dave began to talk about his PT boat service, and to reflect on the impacts his World War II experiences had on his life.*

At the end of the war, I was in a fog. I didn't know what was happening. I didn't really feel comfortable until I got home. I visited an aunt in San Francisco, and she started giving me all this stuff about me being crazy from combat. And I didn't like it, so I left, because I didn't think I was crazy. Maybe I was.

I was at my best in those boats, and I could do anything when I wanted to. And I got very well known. I did so many crazy things that I got a reputation. And even after the war, they'd call me up and say, "Hogan, you got any girls for me?" And I was supposed to have all the girls, and I didn't have all the girls. I had a reputation for having all the girls, but I wasn't quite as good as my reputation. But, I'd get phone calls like that.

When I got out of the service, I was happy not to get any mail or anything from the Navy. I didn't want anything. I'd had it. I had a couple of rules I learned in the Navy. Number one is that the guy above you is always dumber than you are. Number two, I didn't want to get in the Reserves. Some guys made pretty good deals in the Reserves and are still getting a lot of pensions out of it, and all that. I didn't want any of that.

The war gave me some real bad habits. I could have gone and flipped out and been a bum very easy. I enjoyed going out to a bar. It doesn't happen anymore. Bars aren't the same. But I could easily have been a bum. But I went to law school, and we were all from the service. Some of us had good service records, and we outranked all our instructors. And the great thing is that when I started to practice law, everybody tried to help me. It was the greatest feeling I ever had. The judge would take care of my case for me. He'd do anything to help me, because I had come back from the service, and they all knew where I had been, in the Solomons, and everything. The feeling was just tremendous, and it helped me get started. The fact I was on PT boats helped. It was supposed to be the great thing, you know?

One of the three guys who got back to the States before me and had a front cover in *Life* magazine, he committed suicide about twenty years after the war. He was Stilly Taylor, and he was an interesting guy. He was a pretty good PT boat operator, because he was a famous sailor. He was from a very wealthy family. All three of these guys went to Princeton, or some damn place. It was the first time I was ever with that type of person, and, you know, I learned in the Navy that they're no different from anybody else.

Stilly always had woman trouble. He never could handle women. When we were down in Panama, he always had a car or went out with movie starlets that came down there. He had a lot of money, and we were kids! We looked up to him. And he was something. His parents had a big place on Long Island, and all that kind of thing. His brother had a big ranch up near the Montana-Wyoming border, 150,000 acres or something like that. His brother was a great guy. He wasn't in PT boats but was in the Navy. He married a wealthy woman who was interested in horse racing, and she helped him buy that ranch. They had a bunch of kids, and they came from the East and became big shots in the west. I got to meet them all. And I later skied with the brother a lot. He had a house one block away from me in Aspen.

When I came back after the war I started law school. I got back in December, 1945, and I was in law school in January, and I got out of law school in two years. I went summers and got out of law school in record time. Since I went through law school in two years, I didn't have a full opportunity of learning every little thing. It was easy for me, and I never studied. But I made one rule going to school. I never missed a day, no matter how drunk I was the night before. I went every day and listened. But I never did the reading for it. I never prepared for class, and I would sit there and write notes of what I heard. And when I prepared for an exam, I just went through that notebook, and I reduced every case to one or two words. So by remembering those two words, I remembered the bulk of the case, and that was a method I used to get through law school, and it worked like a charm. I was able to review a course in two hours, the whole course, by just opening up the book and looking for the key words that I wrote. It was a damned good technique. It worked. But I never read a case before class. You know, everybody was supposed to do three hours of reading for every class and read all the cases and have ideas, and I never read one. But I listened.

I got paid to go to law school from the GI Bill. And that helped me get a car in a hurry. I also got paid to go to dancing school. This was also one of my Veteran's Benefits, and it was better than paying for it. I didn't turn out to be a very good dancer. The trouble is that when you learn to dance in a dancing school, you're a follower, rather than a leader, if you know what I mean. And you've forever got to try to get over that. I was never a great dancer. But I was a little better than I was in college. They paid for the craziest things.

I had a roommate in college who was over there in PT boats, Kenny Malloy. I knew him a little in college before the war, but he was my roommate in law school after the war. And he had been out in the Pacific over in the New Guinea area, and he was really a tough character. He was an All-American lacrosse player, a little guy, but as tough as nails, and he got a Silver Star, and I'm sure he earned it. We spent a year and a half in law school together. He was a real promoter, and he promoted himself. He was not bashful. He ran professional boxing in Syracuse while we were in law school. He ran it, and I sold the popcorn and peanuts. And we lived in a hotel in downtown Syracuse. So you see I didn't have a lot of time to study, and it was wild. We knew the fellow whose father owned the hotel and we lived in the penthouse, in downtown Syracuse. It was a rough neighborhood, but we didn't know the difference. We had keys to the hotel kitchen. We'd go in and eat any time we wanted to. I'd go in there and make breakfast for myself. And I got that new car and had it there. And we lived, I'll tell you. Every drunk in Syracuse knew of us. We'd go into a bar, put two dollars down on the bar and drink all night. I really don't know how I got through law school, because living with

Kenny was absolutely chaotic. If you wanted to rest, there was no way, because he always had something going. He was nuts. And he became a New York State Supreme Court judge.

We lived together for a year and a half, and we never talked about the war, even though we were both on PT boats. We never mentioned a thing about it. The only thing he told me was that he was going to go into Japan before they actually attacked. He was going to drop off a lot of Special Forces guys to go in on the beach there. And that was his job. He was already on the way to Japan when they dropped that bomb. Both of us got through law school, but I don't know how.

And with everything else we had going on, we finished law school in two years. It's usually a three or three-and-a-half year thing to get through. And usually it would be one hell of a lot of studying. You'd constantly spend your time in the law libraries. And I didn't even know where the library was. You know, the funny thing was, a professor in law school thought he was doing me a favor to ask me a question about condemnation. And I didn't know what he was talking about. And that ended up becoming my specialty in law.

A lot of the guys I was with on PT boats became lawyers for some reason. For instance, this guy Nikoloric was brilliant, he had a good mind. He was probably as smart as anybody I've ever dealt with. He went to Princeton and got to know Searles in school, and all these other people. From college he came to PT boats, and immediately they all helped him. He moved very fast through the ranks. He came home and was one of the heroes right away, as soon as he got home. He decided to go to law school, and he always was involved with a senator or somebody, and he came to take the New York State Bar exam. And it just so happened that I was in the same room that day in Albany to take the Bar exam. He was so bright that I thought he was going to go through this like we used to say in the Navy, "Like shit through geese."

89

Well, he started the exam, and it was a two-day exam. At two o'clock on the second day he left, and I said, "My God, I'm going to flunk this thing." I was only halfway through it and working like hell to get through it. And I worked on until five o'clock that day, and finally quit. It turned out that he flunked the Bar, the New York Bar, because he had spent the preparation for it down in Florida on the beach. So then he finally came back and passed the Bar later. He went into a real famous law firm in Washington, and he got interested in stocks and bonds and promoting that part of the law. He went out West, to the state of Washington, and he was a big-shot lawyer immediately. He then went back to Washington and got into trouble as a lawyer, and he was barred from practicing law before all the government agencies in Washington. He could still practice law, but he couldn't do it in those particular agencies. And that really hurt him. From then on, he went downhill. When I had a case in Washington, I used to stop and see him. I'd have parties and invite him, and, finally, he just died. There's a guy who had so much ability; he had such a great mind, and he had such a great start. There was no limit to what he was going to do. So there's a guy who could've owned Washington, and everything could have worked for him. He had this connection with all the Princeton guys. And they all thought he was a marvel. But it didn't pan out for him because he broke too many rules. I think his failing the New York Bar Exam the first time was an indication of how he did things. He should have been number one.

I never talked about the war, and friends of mine never talked about it. My law school roommate, Kenny Malloy, he was even in PT boats and we never talked about it. And remember my best friend when I was a kid in Rochester, Smitty (Rod Smith), we'd go fishing every summer by ourselves in Canada? Well, I didn't find out until I showed up at his funeral that he had won the Silver Star in the war. I knew he was a Naval officer on a destroyer, the USS *Fletcher*, because one day he showed up at Tulagi to visit me. He found out I was there with the PT boats, and the *Fletcher* was around in the area, so he somehow got over to Tulagi and found me. He was kind of a wild man. After the war he got back to Rochester and got married and had about four kids real quick. He'd go out drinking and show up at my house at 4 a.m., drunk, but he was a good guy. He and his wife bought a brand new house in one of those neighborhoods where everyone had a lot of kids, and sometimes they'd be putting their kids to bed at night and find out they had one of the neighbor's kids. Well, their house was painted white, and he wanted a red house. So he figured he'd buy a couple of cases of beer and invite his friends over to help him paint. This wasn't working out like he'd hoped, since there was more beer drinking than painting going on, and after a few months he didn't even have one side of the house painted. Well, one morning he wanted to go out and play golf, he was a good golfer, but his wife said he had to paint more of the house before he could go out and play. So he gets out there on his ladder with a can of red paint, and he's painting, and the neighbor lady leans out her window and yells at him, saying it's a shame he can't even paint his own house, that he doesn't even have one side done, and by god why doesn't he get it finished. So Smitty very calmly takes his paint brush, and in large red letters on one of the sides facing her house he hadn't painted yet, he writes "fuck you," and then he went out and played golf.

Smitty and I went on fishing trips after the war for years. One trip was to the Thousand Islands area of Lake Ontario to fish for bass. I was never a big bass fisherman, but I went along anyway. We were out on a boat that had two motors, a big one to get you out to where you'd fish, and a small one for trawling. And we had another guy with us who was a carpenter. So one afternoon we're out there and the weather got bad, real bad. And the wind is blowing, and it's raining hard, and big waves came up, and you could see huge rocks exposed by the waves near the shore. Some of the waves would come up over the stern of the boat, it was only about two feet high, and kill the big motor. Well, the carpenter was terrified, but Smitty and I had both been in the Navy, so we were calmly maneuvering the boat. We started the small motor, and it took us hours, from about 7 p.m. to 2:30 a.m., but we finally made it back to the dock. And that motor must have died about fifty times, but Smitty and I had that experience from the Navy, and we'd had to deal with a lot worse during the war.

So I showed up at Smitty's funeral, and I found out for the first time what he did during the war. It turns out that while he was on the *Fletcher*, which was a famous destroyer, the first of the Fletcher-class destroyers, a Japanese bomb hit the ship but didn't explode, and it was embedded in the deck. So Smitty got two other sailors, and they dug that bomb out and tossed it overboard. And he was awarded the Silver Star for that. I had to give a eulogy at the funeral, so I included that story. On all those fishing trips we went on after the war, can you imagine him not mentioning that story? And I only found out about it after he died. But that's how we all were. We never talked about the war.

# 11: SKIING

You know what amazed me? What straightened me out about the whole damn thing? After the war, I went to ski. Just about two years after the war was over I went to Munich. I had just gotten out of law school, and we could ski over there for only two hundred bucks. Later I went to Europe with my wife and daughter one summer. I rented a Volkswagen, and took it all over Europe, and we were down in Palermo, Italy, and all the natives down there came out and spit on the car because it was German. I also skied in Austria, France, and Switzerland for three years in a row after finishing law school. I had great fun and a great deal in Europe, which was very interesting at the end of the war. Most of the remainder of my skiing was in Aspen where I owned two houses. I also did some ski trips to Canada.

I love skiing. When I was an undergraduate I got on the ski team because I had a car. I could drive the other guys to the ski area. I really learned how to ski as a result of getting on the ski team. Well, I raced and I did all that. I was no great racer, but I got a letter for being on the ski team. I got married and went to Aspen, Colorado, on my honeymoon, and this was in 1952. And nobody could believe that I was a honeymooner, because I got up at 8 a.m. the next morning to ski. In about 1960 we bought a lot up on Red Mountain. And I built a little cabin up there. Even then Aspen had a lot of movie stars and authors that came to ski. The author Leon Uris lived about two doors away, and I got to know him very well. The actor Gary Cooper was about three blocks away. I'd drive right past his place when I went down to town.

*Dave skiing in Aspen, Colorado, early 1990s.*

But my wife didn't like driving down that road into Aspen in the snow, and she wanted to live right in Aspen. So I sold that property and bought three lots next to each other in town. Whoever bought my little cabin up on Red Mountain tore it down and built a mansion. The house I built in Aspen was set up for us to come and ski for a few weeks in the winter, and for me to come fish in the summer. We built the living areas for us on the upper floor, and on the ground floor were the garage and an apartment for a caretaker, so we'd have someone living there looking after the place. And this was a fairly small house by Aspen standards now. The assessment for that house in Aspen was high, but the cost was low, giving me a $3 million plus capital gain when I sold it to my neighbor. He wanted to buy it from me. And the crazy thing is that he bought it for all that money and just tore it down to make more open space around his house, and to give him a better view. This is what has happened to Aspen. It used to be that all the celebrities and movie stars and artists and authors would come into town in the evenings and have dinner and drinks, and everyone mingled and had a good time. Now the movie stars come to Aspen and close themselves up in their huge mansions and bring all their friends and a staff of cooks with them, and they never leave their houses. You never see them in town at restaurants or bars any more. And that's a real change from what Aspen used to be like.

*Dave's vacation home in Aspen, Colorado. Note the fish insignia over the balcony at center. He sold the property to his neighbor in 2006, and the house was promptly torn down to make a better view and more open space around his neighbor's home.*

I skied each year until 2006, and I got to know the local people and enjoyed it greatly. During this period, I also had wonderful skiing from a helicopter in British Columbia, where the deep dry snow is the best in the world. I went there with my friend Art Rock, who lived in Aspen and made his living as a business backer of computer companies in California.

I had two close calls from skiing. I got into a group of skiers from Aspen who went to British Columbia each year to ski. On one of those trips, I got into an avalanche. After going to the top of the mountain in the helicopter, I started down behind the Swiss guide, and I followed him right into an avalanche that he had inadvertently triggered. I was able to keep upright while following him down until I got near the end of the avalanche area, where I fell and was covered tightly by snow. They pulled me out, and I immediately got up and left the area. It happened so fast that I still only remember a small amount of what went on while I was going down. The Swiss guide had turned out of the avalanche just as I fell, so he was okay.

My second close call was when our group went up to be dropped off on a mountaintop in Canada in an old Sikorsky helicopter. This helicopter had been in the Seven Day War in Israel, and it still had some bullet holes in the fuselage. It carried twenty people and proved to be too big for the purpose. We reached the top of the mountain on the first attempt, but the helicopter had to turn back because it was too windy to land. The pilot was trying to fly it back down to where we took off, but with the wind and turbulence the helicopter went out of control. In order to get it in its proper attitude, the pilot was going through a procedure of diving the helicopter so that he could try to regain control. He dove the helicopter three times, and on the fourth try he was able to get the helicopter to right itself, only 700 feet from the ground. This was a terrible experience. We were all in there together, all crunched up in the helicopter and wondering if the pilot could get it under control before we crashed. It was a sobering experience that I'll never forget. I didn't ski from helicopters again in that area.

Back in Aspen one time I was with a guide and saw him go down the back of Aspen Mountain, a very steep area out of the ski boundaries. He got ahead of me quite a distance, and then I saw him get caught in an avalanche, and he went down with it and got buried, and I never saw him again. This happened about the first of March, and they didn't find him until the snow melted later that spring.

# 12: PRACTICING LAW

Jack Kennedy and I got along pretty well, and we had long, boring nights to visit out there in the Solomons. After the war, he asked me if I'd help him run for President. At the time I had just started to go into the practice of law, and it looked like his campaign and everything was going to take two years, and I didn't want to spend two years doing that, so I said, "No." So he asked the same question to another guy he'd met before the war in Europe, and he was out there in the Solomons with us as an intelligence officer, a guy named Byron White, "Whizzer" White, the football star from Colorado. Byron White wasn't very friendly, and he didn't want to talk much to anybody. He was kind of a cold fish. When they broke the Japanese code, White was sent to tell us what was happening without us knowing his source. So he kept away from us, and that was part of his job.

Well anyway, Kennedy talked Byron out of his law practice and into helping him run for president. Kennedy won, of course, and Byron got appointed assistant attorney general. And then when there was a Supreme Court opening, Kennedy got him in there. So I guess I blew my chance to be a Supreme Court justice! But I don't have any regrets. I had a great career in law. But it was nice of Kennedy to ask me. I had gotten along with him very well, and I respected him. I thought he was quite a guy.

I went to the Kennedy Inauguration. He invited me and my wife. We saw him for a little while, but he was busy, and there was a snowstorm, and it raised hell with everything. His father was there, and he let it be known he was there, and he was giving just a bit too much support. If his father had let him alone, Kennedy would have never been president. His father had been pro-German for a while and didn't have much of a reputation. Jack had to keep away from him. But his father was in the background of a lot of things, and got him a lot of votes from people like gangsters. We had a bunch of PT guys at the Inauguration, but we never really got together. They had a PT boat they towed through the streets. The people who were in his crew on the 109 were involved in that. But I saw everybody and we had a good time. Homer Facto didn't go. It was too bad. He would have loved it. Most of the ones who came had been with him on the various boats, and some were my crew.

I was at the Inauguration party, and Kennedy and his wife came and I saw him there. I was reminded of when he sort of made an ass of himself when he was running for president. He came to a PT boat reunion and was giving a political speech on how we should run the government. These PT boat guys were just trying to get drunk, and they weren't listening to him. He really didn't go over too great, because they didn't want to hear that stuff. His father thought that the more he had to do with PT boats, the better he should be received. You know, PT boats were given credit for a hell of a lot of stuff they didn't accomplish. PT boats were the thing to do, it was a noted service, but it wasn't as good as they would try to make it out.

I stayed in touch with Kennedy through his Presidency. I used to write him notes. I have several letters from him. I used to call Kennedy at the White House. I could call that secretary of his, Mary Lincoln, and there was a private number I could use to get through. She knew me and the other PT guys, and she'd answer his phone. That's how he knew if a friend sent him a letter or something. She would decide if he got the letter or if he didn't get it. She screened everything.

The day Kennedy got shot I was in New York City to give some kind of speech on a law problem. Late in the morning I heard he was hit, and then later heard he had died. And you know, everything in New York City just stopped. I never gave the speech. I just got on a train and went home. It really hit me. I felt bad. If Kennedy would have stuck to what he had started, it would have been a great thing. I lost a hell of a good friend.

Just before he took that trip to Dallas, I'd had a duplicate made of the commissioning plate I'd taken off the PT 59. I'd turned the 59 over to Kennedy when I left the Solomons, after he lost the 109, and he had another adventure on the 59 after I left. So I figured he'd like a copy of that commissioning plate. I sent it to him at the White House, and I got a phone call from his secretary, Mary Lincoln, telling me he'd received it and would write me a note when he got back from the Dallas trip. Well, he never came back from Dallas, and I never got that note.

Looking back on when Kennedy asked me to get involved in politics, I think now I made the right choice, because I think I could easily have been a very poor politician. I was too frank and too quick to size up something. You know, that's one thing I gained in the service, and I applied it throughout my entire lifetime. I can meet somebody, and I make up my mind right away whether I like them or not. And you figure out how many times you're wrong doing that. But I wasn't wrong too often, and I would meet clients and say, that guy isn't for me. And I'd save myself so much trouble by cutting it off right away. It was one of my best skills in being a lawyer. I would look at a guy, talk to him for a few minutes, and I'd try to make up my mind whether I liked him or not, or whether I could trust him, you know, and all the rest. I made mistakes a couple of times, and I lived to regret it, because you deal with the wrong people and you get yourself in plenty of trouble.

My mother had a stroke when she was fairly young. This happened on the first day I went to work with my father, who was also a lawyer. She had the stroke in the morning, and she was alone on the floor all day. She lived about eight years after the stroke, but she was in pretty rough shape. I built my mother and father a new house using my GI mortgage benefits. After my mother passed away, through the rest of my adult life, I was dealing just with my father.

He was a help and he got me started, but he was a self-made man, and he was not the kind of person who could be my partner. My father started out very poor, and he earned his living the hard way. He went to law school by selling newspapers and candy on trains; they called them "news butchers." And he used to go to New York and then come back, and go to law school in Syracuse, and he was brilliant at it. And he could even remember cases by name, age, date, page number, and volume. He was really brilliant, but he was very difficult, very difficult.

During my first case in the Supreme Court, my father sat next to me to attempt to help me. And there's a jury there, and I'm doing what I should be doing. The other lawyer was a well-trained old-timer, and he sat with his hand on my witness, which my father thought was distracting my witness, and I should object. I didn't think so, and I didn't object. Finally, he pulled my arm and screamed out so everybody in the courtroom heard, including the judge and jury. "Object, object . . . he's pissing all over you." I won the case because the jury felt sorry for me, but that was the last time I let him come to the courtroom with me. I gave up a lot of opportunities to stay with him, but it was murder. I was in business with him until he died, in about 1986 or something like that.

Once my father was called in for a very important case, and he asked me to help him, because he was unable to handle the judge. The opposing trial lawyers were the best in the city of Rochester. At that time I was new in the law, with little experience. My father got in this position because he asked our friend, the CCC boxer from Syracuse I mentioned before who got to be a Supreme Court judge, what the trial judge thought of his brief that he worked hard on and just filed. Our friend said, "He threw it in the shithouse." My father was so upset that he couldn't face the judge or the opposition, so I had to take over.

When he got older the real reason he came to the office was to play Solitaire or to talk to the staff. He was absolutely disruptive, but it kept him there. And when he died he left me his library, which I paid for, and his pending cases, of which he had none.

I did very well in my practice of the law. I got to be a specialist in condemnation cases. The reason for condemnation cases was the lack of good transportation in the cities run by private operators. The federal government supplied the money, including buses, to improve mass transportation. The assets of the private companies would be purchased by condemnation by the government if the private companies were failing to properly handle the needs of the public. The private owners sold their assets in condemnation even though these assets were losing money. The bus companies were taken over and operated by the local governments, resulting in a ruling that the proper valuation method for valuing these assets taken was reproduction new less depreciation, even though the bus companies were losing money and would have little economic value otherwise. This was determined in the Fifth Avenue Bus Company case in the City of New York, which was accepted as the ruling all over the country.

I therefore mostly represented private owners, but also represented two public owners, the Rochester bus company and the Washington,

D.C., bus company. I tried the cases to get the best settlement for the companies that were being condemned. I used engineers to testify as to the value of the bus and trolley companies for the case in Rochester. I got along well with them, and when they got called to testify in other cases, they'd recommend me.

During the cases, I took testimony from the expert witnesses on both sides, transcribing their testimony. And then I'd read their testimony and learn that they were often inconsistent with what they said before. I had good luck with the inconsistencies. If I found inconsistencies, I got good results in my valuations. But I had to read and read to prepare for these cases. I'd stay up all night.

I went all over the country trying these cases, and it was fun. I tried one in Denver, a big case where the company had a trolley company and then a bus company, and I represented the owners. In Denver, it was like a small town at the time I worked for the bus company. The group also owned the football team, the sugar beet operation, the railroad, and the national bank. They were nice people, but they had no regard for new people. They controlled the construction of many new buildings by controlling the water supply in the city, so that new competition could not come into town. They knew people all over the state of Colorado, and people in Aspen that I knew. They didn't want me to try the case very strenuously, because they thought that a large award would affect their position with the local people. They didn't need the money, so I got an award for them, but it wasn't as big as it should have been. They gave me five-gallon cans of gasoline from their ranches when I drove home to Rochester, because that was the time of the oil shortage in the early 1970s. They were not very worldly, but they sure knew how to make money. It was interesting to represent this group. I learned a lot about business from them.

And then I did a case in Milwaukee. I did two in Minneapolis, and then went all over the country for the cases that followed. There were the same experts in every case. I'd get the transcript from one case, take it to next, and I had big boxes of transcripts. I went across the whole country doing that for six years. One of the last cases was in Washington, D.C. I was made a Special Assistant U.S. Attorney, and I represented the government in the condemnation of a bus company. I lived in the Watergate Hotel. I would entertain my friends, and the government paid for all my parties. I could have any parties I wanted, and have the bill as high as I wanted. They wouldn't give me a high enough amount of money for the legal work, but they paid for the parties. I had to explain that to a woman who came to investigate why it was such a large amount. I was still operating. Operating in the Justice Department was just like operating in the Navy.

I had a great time in Washington. I was there for a year and a half. When I got into the Justice Department, I had a case where the owner was asking for $200 million, and I settled it for $60 million in the federal district court after trying it twice. And they were very happy with that. In the next courtroom the famous Watergate case was being tried, which ended in President Nixon leaving office. All this was very interesting to me. The lawyers trying the case were friendly, and I talked to them often.

When I was doing the condemnation cases, I was all over the country. It was like a traveling circus. It was really interesting in that every place was different in the way they practiced law. And I learned how to do it in a foreign atmosphere. What I did was, I hired local lawyers to work with me, but I ran the case. And I learned a hell of a lot. I could've gotten jobs with huge law firms with great reputations but I didn't, and I stayed with my father. But I got away from Rochester by doing the condemnation cases.

I was successful in trying other types of cases as a result of my experience in the condemnation cases, in working for the federal government and other local governments, and in the U.S. Attorney General's office, and I used my lack of respect for the quality of their work in regard to my future cases. These government legal operations were being poorly run and managed during my experience. I never over-estimated the quality of their work. It helped contribute to my success. These cases resulted in my legal activity after finishing the bus condemnation cases and were in three categories. They were involved in valuation cases where the IRS was involved, as well as in bank fraud cases and in real estate valuation for local taxes. I got involved in some interesting cases. One was the valuation of the A & P Companies grocery chain regarding school taxes they were supposed to pay based on the valuation of the size of their building. They were located near Elmira, New York, and their building was reputed to be the biggest single-story building in New York State, which was used for distributing groceries to its stores in the eastern United States. It was something like 100 acres under one roof. In another case I represented the town of Gates in Monroe County, where there was a huge new, modern Eastman Kodak Company plant. I also represented the town of Webster in the valuation of a Xerox plant. I won all these cases, with the exception of the A & P case.

An important IRS case was the one I tried in Buffalo in federal court with the aid of Sherm Levey. He was an expert in IRS law, in which I had no expertise. I tried the case, and we won it even though the IRS was trying to make an example of our client, a road contractor in the Buffalo area. The government spent three years investigating this case, with two agents spending most of the time at our client's office in coming up with a charge of over 100 counts against him. He was charged with illegally using cash in his business. As a result, our luck in clearing him of all charges was that the government greatly over-tried the case. We proved many of the excess efforts were not called for.

Back when I was trying the first valuation case that I had in Rochester, I called a witness from Philadelphia. The next day we were having dinner and he said to me, "Do you have cable in Rochester?" And I said, "What's cable? I've never heard of it." He says, "Cable TV. It's a great thing. Why don't you see if you can get into it?" The next day I got together with two other guys, and we got the cable company for Monroe County in the Rochester area.

We owned it for about six years, and we eventually sold it to Time-Life, and it got to be something. But at first I didn't have faith in it. When we started it, I was building this house and needed all the money I could get together to build it. But there were the two other guys with me who really had a lot of faith in me and the cable TV company. I didn't know if it was going to make it or not. It was iffy. So I didn't put a lot of money into it. The other guys put in more, so they had a bigger return when we sold it.

We called it People's Cable Company, because we tried to make it into a friendly people's corporation rather than a large impersonal business venture. There were also a lot of these companies that were shady. There was a lot of political activity to get those franchises. So that's where "People's . . ." came from; we tried to make it close to the people and away from the big corporations. We really did think that way. We could have made it much bigger if we had wanted to play ball and started to grow and let other people run it. But the politics got terrible, and we wouldn't have anything to do with it. We decided to sell those franchises.

We got so that we knew what we were doing. Time-Life was building a cable system right near us. It cost them, like, millions to start it, and we did it for a few hundred thousand dollars. In order to get the franchise, we had to have twenty customers in each town. So during that winter, I went skiing in Aspen and those two guys worked like hell. We sold it later to Time-Life for $35 million. It's the only business I've ever entered.

That was in about 1975. My part of that $35 million has allowed me to go fishing all over the world. Each year I went to Alaska, Canada, western U.S., South America, New Zealand, and Russia. I saw beautiful countries and caught great fish.

I got to know important fishing guides who were experts in their area. They brought me to the best places to fish, and to catch record fish. One was a 32-pound brown trout.

*After the war Dave went on fishing trips all over the world. Here is a catch of Atlantic salmon in the early 1980s before the catch-and-release program was started. Photo was taken near the George River in northern Canada north of Hudson Bay. From left to right, Dave Levy, Mrs. Lewis (her family business supplied the New York Times with paper), and Rod "Smitty" Smith, Dave's friend from childhood.*

*Dave caught this brown trout in New Zealand in 2001. Fishing guide John Grimmel is at left, Dave at right.*

*A record setting 32 pound female brown trout caught by Dave on the Rio Grande River in Tierra Del Fuego, southern Argentina, in 2003.*

# 13: REFLECTIONS

What bothered me about the war and still bothers me is that everybody thinks it's glamorous and everybody thinks it's efficient. It's the least efficient type of activity I've ever been a part of. And if you're a thinking person and you're out there and you're seeing what's going on; you know, you can't understand it. We were doing what we were told to do, and we did it. But I didn't know that it was such an important event.

I never smoked. I lost two wives who smoked. I had malaria and dengue fever. I got dengue fever in Guadalcanal and got rid of it fairly easy. But I was sick as hell with malaria. I got that in the Philippines. I was taking Atabrine—we were all yellow with that—and I still got malaria, and it lasts for a lifetime. But I was lucky after the war, because I never had any trouble with nightmares. Maybe that's because I had this bad attitude. I mean, I treated the whole thing like it was a joke. The only trouble I've had was hearing, and I still have problems with that. I lost 30 percent of my hearing from the noise of the engines on the boat, and gunfire I guess. As a lawyer, when I'm trying a case I use hearing aids. But I'm able to get along without hearing aids most of the time. I hate them, so I don't wear them. But if I go to a PT boat convention, everybody's wearing hearing aids. Out in the Pacific, they didn't tell us anything about how all that noise on the boats would ruin your hearing.

I attended PT boat reunions for years. Those reunions weren't much about history, and we didn't think of ourselves as a veterans group. It was a drinking club. We used to have our get-togethers at the New York Yacht Club. The first time I went, we all stayed up all night. And, gradually, with each successive year, we went to bed earlier. And, finally, the last time, we all went to bed at 10:30 p.m.

The war really changed my whole life. Before I went to the Pacific, I wasn't real motivated, and I didn't really know what I was going to do in life. But after my experiences in the Navy, I came back with a real sense of self-confidence. I'd had to get along with and deal with all types of people, and I'd had to run a PT boat and have that responsibility, and I'd taken that boat and my crew out in stressful situations under fire, and I was able to do it and, I think, was pretty good at it, and that builds your self-confidence. I'd have never gotten that range of experience if I hadn't been in the service. I got out of the Navy, and I just felt like I had the confidence that I could do anything, and let's get to it! I'd done that legal exercise right at the end, in the Philippines, that got me interested in law, and with the GI Bill I got my law degree after the war.

Being a trial lawyer required me to have all the responsibility of a case, and in that way it was different from being the skipper of a small boat during the war. On a small boat the skipper was dealing with fifteen people in making many of his decisions. I prefer the position of a trial lawyer over that of a PT boat skipper, because it's easier to control yourself than fifteen other people who never think alike. As a trial lawyer, if someone takes advantage of you in a case, you quite often have the opportunity of outworking him in the next case, and can straighten out your standing.

That Jewish business made it difficult for me. I overcame most of that, and I really got to be a fairly good lawyer. I got to be really high in my category as a lawyer, and I was trying 200 million dollar cases for the government. But the Navy helped me a hell of a lot. I never gave the Navy credit for that, but the fact was that I made it in the Navy, and I got on an even keel with all those hotshot guys. At first they didn't pay any attention to me at all, and then they did when I made a name for myself in the Pacific. And then they all respected me afterward for what I was doing in the law. I used to see Hugh Robinson and those guys in Washington, D.C., and they were wonderful and encouraged my progress in the law.

Some of the PT boat guys I knew have gone back to the Solomons, but not very many. I mean, most of them feel like I do: to hell with that place! I don't want to ever see it again. The food was terrible, the jungle and climate were terrible, and who the hell wants to go back and see it. But I'll never forget what happened to me out there. My life was never the same, and I believe the war in the islands changed me for the better.

I have had an enjoyable and successful life practicing law. I get to the office in the mornings, and I'm now ninety (August 2008). I skied until I was eighty-seven, and still fish all over the world. I fish from boats because I've had Parkinson's for the last thirteen years. It's a debilitating disease, but my luck continues because this disease is not progressing at the usual rate. It has slowed but not stopped, but it has not prohibited me from enjoying life. I was also very lucky to have wonderful medical care from doctors at the University of Rochester Strong Memorial Hospital, because they were experts in treating Parkinson's. They kept me from the extremes of the disease and in action up till now.

I've traveled all over the world on wonderful trips, like going around the world on a private French Concorde on the millennium (January 1,

2000) with seven stops in fourteen days, including Hawaii, Sydney, Hong Kong, India, Africa (Serengeti in central Africa and Egypt), France, and New York. The Concorde traveled across the Atlantic Ocean in three and a half hours but didn't carry fuel enough to go farther, so more stops were required for fuel. Therefore, you never get tired of flying in the Concorde, because no matter how far it goes, it stops every three or four hours. It flew at a speed greater than the speed of sound. It's great because of that. It was a wonderful experience. I also flew the Concorde home from Europe after taking the ship *Queen Elizabeth II* across the Atlantic. I also flew it to Europe to take the Orient Express.

I have a physical therapist named David Millard, and his nine-year-old son Christopher got interested in my war experiences. A short version of my story was published in a book called *Pacific War Stories* in 2004, so I lent Christopher the book and he read my story. Then he wrote to tell me what he thought. I think it's a great letter, and it shows you that another generation is interested in what happened during World War II. Here's part of the text of the letter:

*"Mr. Levy's PT boat was about 70 feet long and could travel at about 55 knots, or 60 mph. These boats were made of wood—that's why they were so fast. There were times during the war when Capt. Levy was afraid, but he still had to do his job. He and his crew once had only 'spam' to east for three months. Spam is a yucky canned meat. Mr. Levy was friends with John F. Kennedy, who at that time was also a PT captain. Mr. Levy wished he could have made the PT boats safer for the crew. He wanted them to have more protection around them. I am very lucky because my dad is a friend of Mr. Levy, and I was able to meet him and interview him. He let me come to his house and told me all kinds of stories. He even showed me some pictures. We sat in his kitchen and drank hot chocolate and ate cake. We talked about the Navy and fishing. He really likes to fish, and he showed me all his gear. He has fished all over the world, and his biggest fish was 32 pounds. My mom said that to meet Mr. Levy was going back in time and touching history. I*

*asked Mr. Levy if he thinks he is a hero, and he said "NO" right away. I think he is a hero because he had to go to war and was brave enough to say that sometimes he was afraid, and he wished for safer boats for his crew, not just a wish for himself. I really like visiting with Mr. Levy, because I was able to meet a real hero and make a new friend."*

Now, isn't that a great letter? And remember, it was written by a nine-year-old kid. It's pretty good, isn't it?

I've changed my mind about the benefits I gained from my duties in the U.S. Navy. I now believe that it helped me a lot in my life. Hard work as a lawyer brings results to you much quicker than it does in the Navy. And as a lawyer, your achievements are seen by everyone as your individual abilities create results. My greatest pleasure in practicing law is to be walking down one side of the street and the lawyer on the other side of the street is telling his friend, "There goes Dave Levy, he's a pretty good lawyer." I was a better lawyer than I was a PT skipper, but I was extremely lucky as a PT skipper.

When I look back on my experiences in the Navy, I realize now that the guys who were my fellow PT boat skippers had been raised to be gentlemen, and that was quite a bit different from how I was raised. They were all different from me, and initially I hated them for that. They had gone to prep schools, the Naval Academy, or Ivy League colleges. I hung around with gangsters when I was a kid, and I scraped by in college at Syracuse. So here were these cultured and refined gentlemen, and I didn't want to be a gentleman. I wanted to be tough like my father, but I found out I couldn't get along being tough. Hugh Robinson and Mark Wertz were the two who had the most positive influence on me. They made me semi-normal, and I owe them a lot. I was fighting a battle where there was no battle, and they made me realize they weren't against me. I learned how to get along, and I made a name for myself. To them I was "Hogan," and I was an operator, but I figured out how to get along with those guys even though I had so little in common with them. I got to be great friends with some of them. I ran into the right people at the right times. They helped me greatly in overcoming my various problems. I found out there are real people who forget prejudices and help others make their way in life.